Tailoring
obsessions

Simon
Crompton

Simon Crompton is an author and journalist, and a leading expert on bespoke menswear. His website, Permanent Style, was founded in 2006 and has been named by *GQ*, *The Times* and *The New York Times* as one of the best menswear sites in the world. He is a contributor to the *Financial Times*, *The Rake* and *The Robb Report*, and has written two previous books: *Best of British* and *The Finest Menswear in the World*.

Tailoring

obsessions

Simon
Crompton

hardie grant books

Contents

Why be obsessed with tailoring?

A well-fitting suit is incredibly flattering, but there is a lot of ignorance among men about how to get one. Ready to wear is under used; made to measure is ignored; bespoke is misunderstood. It's not hard to become educated about tailoring however, all you need is a little passion.

A well-made suit can change the way you feel about yourself – a suit tailored to your unique physique means the fit will be perfect and comfortable. A bespoke suit flatters all shapes. It can make you look thinner, fitter and stronger. Some tailors will give the jacket a sharply cut waist yet retain a little 'drape' in the chest, diminishing the former and exaggerating the latter. The V of the chest will accentuate your shoulders and suggest athletic shape, and can increase your confidence, just by looking in the mirror.

Bespoke also allows you to design your own clothes. It means you can put your personality into what you wear. Whether that's the subtle touches of brown horn buttons and turn-ups, or the loud flair of pink pinstripes and lime-green lining, it is personal and unique to you. There are a lot of options out there on the high street, but each is more a question of copying someone else's ideas than coming up with your own. And there's always the risk that you will see 'yourself' coming towards you down the street, wearing exactly the same suit.

▶ A double-breasted chalkstripe suit, made bespoke at Thom Sweeney in London.

Bespoke isn't just for suits. My tailor has made cycling jerseys, cropped jackets and capes, to name a few. It's limited only by what you can imagine. Of course, suits make up the majority of bespoke clothing and most of this book will be concerned with them. But many of the principles, from cloth selection to tips on the fitting process, apply equally well to other types of dress. A great suit is always worth investing in, whether bespoke or not. For the most important times of your life, it gives you and your attire a sense of occasion. It is smart, sleek and serious. If worn every day in the office, it will become a stamp of quiet authority that stays with you through the week, and with others. It can affect how they see you.

For modern man, dressing well is a source of unexplored pleasure; clothes are the last area where he feels he cannot be seen to be making an effort. So he doesn't. That's his first mistake. The effort should never be seen, whether you're into clothes or not. The best style is casual, easy, nonchalant. It should just look like something you threw on in the morning. And such is the quality of your wardrobe and your accumulated taste that it may actually be what you just threw on that morning.

Tailoring can be scary. It's not easy to know how to describe what you want or whether you're getting value for money. That anxiety is dispelled by knowledge, which is what this book endeavours to provide. Whether you're bespeaking a whole new suit or just having some jeans altered, the facts you need are here.

Tailors are wonderfully old-fashioned, which means they create suits that last as well as those of a century ago; and they will fit better than anything else. (However, it does make their language a little antiquated. I have even heard one use 'bespoke' in its original meaning, as a piece of cloth that was 'bespoken' for.) One thing that all Savile Row tailors, and many others besides, insist on is calling the top half of a suit, the 'coat'. Historically, this is correct. That's why we have overcoats – they were worn over the coat. Today, however, an overcoat has been shortened to a coat and a coat is universally referred to as a jacket. Because of this universal recognition, I will refer to this item of clothing as a jacket throughout this book. Tailors will hate me for it. But this book is for you, not them.

▲ Bespoke isn't just for suits. For a modern man, a bespoke sports jacket can often be more useful.

1

Fundamentals

Ready to wear, made to measure and bespoke

The difference between the three main categories of suit – ready to wear, made to measure and bespoke – is really about fit. A bespoke suit might be better made than one that is ready to wear, but this is not always the case.

▲ A basted jacket ready for the first fitting.

Italian houses such as Kiton and Brioni make ready-to-wear (RTW) suits that are superior in quality to some off-Savile Row tailors. So, as much as people include hand construction in the definition of bespoke, it's best to think of it as a question of fit. It's possible to achieve a generally good fit with RTW – the key is to understand the sizing, shop around and have the suit altered if needed.

Made to measure (MTM) takes standard sizes and adjusts them in more ways than you would ever bother to do with an alterations tailor. The suit will likely be made by a machine in the same factory as RTW. It isn't quite bespoke, but it will fit you very well. The advice on both being measured for a MTM suit and selecting its design are similar to bespoke, and almost equally as important.

Bespoke tailoring is different in one key way – the pattern is yours and yours alone. Once the tailor has taken your measurements (around 12–15 normally), he will translate them onto a unique pattern. He will take a piece of brown paper and mark out a

chest piece using your measurements and figuration – everything about the shape of a man that is not expressed in simple measuring, such as the balance of your shoulder blades, hips or stoop. The paper pattern is what defines bespoke; it is more personal and precise than any other form of suit-fitting. It is used to cut sections of cloth that will be 'basted' together (sewn using loose, long stitches that can easily be pulled out) and hung on the customer at his first fitting. At this basted fitting the tailor will chalk on many little changes and alterations, pull out the basting stitches and re-cut the cloth to this new shape. The paper pattern will also be adjusted accordingly, by either taping on or cutting off slivers of paper. These levels of attention are what distinguish RTW, MTM and bespoke: mass production, individual production or painstaking paper.

▲ A suit pattern being marked out at Huntsman, London.

The Italian influence

Possibly the biggest effect on how sartorialism is viewed today comes from the influence of the Italians in the latter half of the twentieth century. Everyone thinks the Italians look good; they are a daily inspiration the world over.

Where the English gentleman might generally experiment with relatively hidden items of clothing – red socks, brightly striped shirts, amusingly patterned braces – among his standard attire of dark suit, black shoes and club tie, the Italian keeps these consistent. He wears a blue shirt and navy tie a lot of the time, allowing him to wear more flannel, linen and coloured shoes.

I coined the phrase 'Italian background' several years ago to describe this blue shirt/blue tie combination, as it is an ideal, neutral background for experimentation elsewhere. In the summer in Milan you will see far more men wear tan linen suits than ever in London, but wearing an Italian background underneath that linen suit somehow makes the whole ensemble look conservative.

▶ Gianni Agnelli (seen here in 1975) was admired for melding strict conservatism with personal quirks, such as wearing his watches on the outside of his shirt.

Sprezzatura

The Italian style icons tend to be those that follow this look and then add small innovations of their own. But these are innovations more deliberately casual than the English. They express *sprezzatura*

– a practiced carelessness, that characterizes their individual style.

The Italians had one man that stood head and shoulders above all other style icons. His name was Gianni Agnelli. Long the CEO of Fiat and a man of politics as well as business, Agnelli was admired for his ability to meld strict conservatism with personal quirks that everyone seemed to notice apart from him.

Agnelli wore his watches on the outside of his shirt cuff. He claimed this was because the band of the watch irritated his skin. Perhaps. But there had to be other types of strap that would not irritate. No, he wore his watch over his cuff because he tried it once (for whatever reason) and liked the style. So he did it again and again until it felt natural. Until it was, and everyone would see that it was.

He wore a lot of flannel. He wore a lot of woollen ties. He famously patronized the Tod's winter boot when one was sent to him by an enterprising Diego Della Valle. But in every photo of the great man he looks serious, business-like, conservative, and his quirks do not undermine that; he is not wearing braces with little pheasants on them, as Englishmen are unfortunately wont to do.

Royal influence

The story of the suit is largely an English story, driven by the role of empire, commerce and cultural colonialism. And in England, the main players were often princes.

Modern men may wonder why royalty made such an impact on the world of menswear. One reason is certainly that they were revered and looked up to. Once a prince had worn it, you had confidence wearing an otherwise daring piece of clothing. But an equally important reason was that people saw pictures of royalty far more than anyone else. With little advertising, magazines or alternative celebrities, royal members were the only pin-ups available. If one of them had genuine character and style, their lasting fame was inevitable.

King Edward VII helped create the dinner jacket as an alternative for evening wear. He brought back the black Homburg hat from Germany, favoured turn-ups on trousers and allegedly left the bottom button of his waistcoat undone after a large repast, which spawned a trend.

His grandson, the Duke of Windsor (right), also had a number of stylistic innovations: belts with trousers, rather than braces; zip flies rather than buttons; and, most famous of all, a more relaxed tailoring pioneered by Frederick Scholte – now known as the London cut, or the drape.

Classic suit styles

▼ Left: One-button single breasted jacket with peaked lapels. Right: Three-button jacket with natural roll and notched lapels.

Most men have a pretty good idea what a suit looks like. In their mind, it will be single breasted, have two or three buttons and notch lapels, and the trousers will sit on the hips and probably not have pleats or turn-ups. But many will be unlikely to manage to describe the suit in these terms. So when presented with the question 'what style of suit would you like?' by their tailor, they will struggle.

Before you can answer that question with confidence, you have to be able to understand some key points of reference, and the advantages of a double-breasted suit, cuffs or pleats, so that you can make your choices accordingly, and know exactly what you want before you attempt to describe it.

Let's start with a single-breasted jacket. The first thing to decide on is the number of buttons, which is more complicated than it sounds and drives other decisions. Then, consider ways to flatter your shape – everyone has something they would rather accentuate or hide.

▼ Left: Two-button single-breasted jacket with notched lapels Right: Double-breasted jacket with peak lapels.

The importance of buttons

Fashions exist even within classic menswear, and over the decades the dominant number of buttons has varied between one, two, three and even four. But the reign of the first and last of those was quite brief – generally the most common style has either been a two- or three-button front.

At the start of the 21st century, three buttons were definitely most fashionable. But there are true three buttons and three buttons that 'roll'. A true three-button jacket will have lapels that end, abruptly, just above the top of those buttons. When only the waist button (the middle one of the three) is fastened, this short lapel will create a sharp, awkward angle at the top of the jacket's front. It has been designed to button the top two, and looks odd if they are both unfastened.

Most other jackets will have some amount of roll to them, so that when the top button is unfastened, the lapel rolls back and lengthens, ending somewhere above the waist button. The ease of the roll will depend on the canvassing of the chest and the tension of the collar.

▲ A one-button flannel suit in airforce blue.

High fastenings (which three or four buttons naturally demand) look good on fewer people, as they shorten the plunge of the lapel and reduce that uniquely elongating, strengthening effect of a good jacket. Nevertheless the style has been popular in the past when driven by specific fashions, such as the Mods or the Teddy Boys in England. And indeed both of those inherited parts of their look from earlier

gentleman's attire where as little shirting was on display as possible – leading to the necessity of a high-fastening jacket or an ever-present waistcoat.

▲ The number of buttons on a jacket is a more complicated choice than it might sound and drives many other decisions.

So you might want to eschew a true three-button jacket in favour of the more natural 'three-rolls-to-two' style, which is both more flexible and flattering than its peers. This will be less of a problem in the US, which has always favoured more relaxed and less structured jackets. The higher fastening, being tighter, buttoned up and necessarily of a narrower cut, has historically found more favour in fashion in France and Italy. If you're going with three buttons, make sure they roll.

Fewer buttons

As we have seen, a higher fastening is less flattering
and, generally, less stylish, and fewer buttons both
lengthens a man and emphasizes his shoulders. You
could be forgiven for thinking that the choice of one
button or two takes this argument a step further,
but in fact the lapel length will likely be the same.
With both styles, the waist button is the top (or only)
fastening – the two-button style merely adds another,
lower button.

What's more, most two-button jackets are designed
for the bottom button not to be done up. You
can fasten it, unlike the bottom buttons of some
waistcoats, but the cut is far more elegant without.
(Some styles have two buttons that sit above and
below the waist, and are designed to both be
fastened. JFK was famously pictured in a couple. But
these are rare, often fashion ephemera, and blunter
than a traditional shape. After all, why turn that
single-point fulcrum into a static bar?)

The second button

So, you may well ask, what is the point of a second
button? It seems redundant. Many commentators
have shared this view, alleging that one button looks
more stylish and three more practical, while a two-
button jacket is just dull. There are three principal
reasons for adding the second button. The first is
practical – a little wind can turn your jacket fronts
inside out, flapping them around and forcing you
to repress them with your hands. That's not exactly
elegant and ruins whatever silhouette was intended

by the cut. The second is a matter of style: one button is sharp, singular, not to say rakish. Dashing to some, louche to others, it is certainly a statement. No matter the jacket's heritage – coming from the morning coat and riding wear – nor its superb modern manifestation (thanks to Huntsman and latterly Richard Anderson), this is a style. And some men don't want a style – they want normal, they want unobtrusive, they want stolid. They do not want anything that could suggest a rake. For them, the two-button jacket is flattering and practical.

Finally, and perhaps least importantly for today's man and style trends, a one-button jacket often looks best with high-waisted trousers. Back when all men wore braces, their trousers all started around their belly button, so the waist of the trousers and of the jacket were both at the same point. This meant that when they put their hands in their pockets, pulling apart the jacket, no shirting was on display. While this isn't necessarily recommended for every modern man, a triangle of puffy shirt is hardly flattering and negates the upward-sweeping triangle of the lapels.

So as a one-button jacket means more of a cutaway front, there is more potential for displaying your waist in this way. Trousers on the natural waist are not required, but the argument for them strengthens. And few men wear trousers of that height today. One versus two buttons is a matter of personality, but consider the arguments on both sides.

Peak lapels

The peak lapel comes from the morning coat that was the standard dress for Victorians in England and formal attire for decades afterwards.

A dinner jacket should have peaked lapels because it is a descendant of the morning coat, the tails being lopped off to make the look more casual. Equally, the often overlooked 'stroller' jacket style also has peaked lapels. This is a black jacket without tails and without

the silk facings of a dinner jacket, but often worn formally with grey trousers and made from a luxurious cloth such as cashmere.

There is nothing necessarily wrong with peaked lapels on a single-breasted suit jacket. Just bear in mind that they are more formal and rakish than notch lapels, and should be treated as such.

Reconsider a double breast

Some men prefer a double-breasted jacket because it can add width to slimmer shoulders. However, this does not have to be the only effect. Much of the impact is a result of design that can be personalized; the position of the buttons, and their number, makes a big difference, for example. A double-breasted front creates immediate width because the foreparts cross over each other rather than joining together. So the lapel runs at an angle across the body, and is usually peaked – accentuating the diagonal. The buttons also create width because they run horizontally as well as vertically.

That squareness and width can easily be mitigated. First, the line of the lapel can be altered radically by the position of the waist button and how far the two foreparts cross over. Imagine a standard double-breasted jacket. Now move the waist button (normally in the middle row of a six-button front, or the top row of a four-button) slowly down. Notice how the slope of the lapel lessens – as the top is fixed at the collar, but the bottom is moving downwards, the line has to straighten up. Now gradually reduce the overlap, so the waist button moves towards the centre of the jacket. Again this straightens the lapel (though also shortening it slightly). Don't push this too far, but you'll be amazed what a difference just an inch or even a half-inch makes.

So when you are having a bespoke suit made, consider the position of the waist button and the extent of the overlap. You can even go for a 6x2 or 4x2

design, where only the bottom buttons look like they fasten. The first of these is not to everyone's taste and can look bulky, but the second is definitely an option with a four-button front. They're also hard to find in the shops today, so it highlights a bespoke design.

Reducing the number of buttons helps, too. Four buttons will look less bulky than six, or you can just have two. This last option looks more fashionable than traditional, but then you can always add more buttons later – another advantage of bespoke. Also, a large man can wear double-breasted much more easily if he reduces its bulk in every other way, through lack of clutter, texture and excess cloth. Large men shouldn't be scared of a double-breasted suit, and slim men should positively embrace it.

▲ A 6x4 double-breasted suit in grey flannel, worn with an olive-coloured silk tie and white linen handkerchief.

Choosing a shape

The subtleties of a suit's design can make a disproportionate difference to how it flatters your figure. Tall or short, broad or narrow, even average build, there are things you should consider whether buying a suit or commissioning bespoke.

Flatter a shorter stature

To increase the appearance of your height, you need to avoid any excess cloth, as this will add to your bulk and emphasize a shorter stature, so go with a close fit.

On the jacket, go for one button, or two maximum. The more buttons there are, the more horizontal points break up the front of the jacket, and, probably more importantly, the shorter the lapels have to be. The sweep of a suit's lapel from neck to waist is the strongest line in the suit and potentially its most flattering. So keep that line as long as possible if you want to appear taller. The difference between one and two buttons is small, as the waist button will not move much with the addition of a button below it.

The jacket's waist should be quite tight, or 'suppressed', in line with the theme of keeping cloth to a minimum. The waist of the trousers, meanwhile, should be high and at a man's natural waist (around the belly button, if not higher). This may feel unnatural to some, but it does make the legs appear

▶ A shorter man benefits from a neat fit and long, clean lines.

longer and produce cleaner lines in the pleats as they drop over the hipbone. If you go for a lower rise, make sure you have slim legs and sharp creases on the trousers.

The jacket should be relatively short in order to, again, lengthen the legs. Nothing is worse for a short man than a jacket that swamps him, whether on the arms, waist or hips. High vents will add to the impression of height; though if you can resist the urge to put your hands in your pockets, a ventless jacket is even better.

Anything that removes bulk from the look of the suit is also beneficial. So avoid ticket pockets, large pocket flaps, patch pockets, pocket handkerchiefs and cuffs on either the sleeves or trousers. They all interrupt the long, clean lines we're aiming for. If the notch in the lapel can be a little higher, that will also help.

Think of bulk when choosing the cloth as well: darker, finer wools will create a sharp silhouette. You should avoid pale tones,

bright colours and large patterns (particularly checks), although a fine pinstripe can elongate your shape. As to the rest of the outfit, dark shoes and a simple tie will accentuate the look, and avoid the contrast of sports jackets or odd waistcoats.

Interrupt a tall man

Now reverse all that for a tall man. Interrupt the look at every possible opportunity: ticket pockets, patch pockets, broad checks and odd jackets. Wear a belt, have trouser cuffs and buy some brogues – the more texture the better. Throw the eye sideways with a pocket handkerchief; eschew a smooth silk tie; wear a waistcoat; wear a watch; have your sleeves a touch shorter so there is always a half-inch of shirt cuff – anything to break up the lines.

Tall men and narrow men have the same tools at their disposal. The thin

▲ Breaking up the appearance of a taller man, here with buttons and belt, reduces the impact of his height.

should ape the tactics of the tall man, the large man those of the short. If you are tall and stout, or thin and short, consider your priorities and apply accordingly. Men generally to want to avoid the latter of those two pairs most.

How to pick colour

For business or generally formal suits, colour is pretty simple, but there are a few ways to make sure you're getting it just right.

The standard colours are blue and grey, and for good reason: no other colours can both look smart and flatter a man's skin tone at the same time. Black is too harsh; brown isn't smart enough; tan is downright casual.

The colour needs to be dark to be businesslike, but that doesn't mean it should be almost black. Navy is the classic blue for business suits – while a dark shade, it is easily distinguishable from black, and is definitely blue. Too many men buy suits that are too dark (closer to midnight blue, a tone often used for eveningwear and which looks black until closely inspected), and make them look pale and pasty. Real blues and greys are much kinder.

A navy or mid-blue is also far more interesting in terms of colour combinations. Midnight blue looks very smart with a white shirt and black shoes, but that's about it. Navy, on the other hand, also looks good with those accessories, but brings out chocolate-brown shoes as well. And a blue shirt provides a great background for experimentation with colour in the tie or handkerchief – strong colours against black just look cheap. Royal blue or cerulean are

▲ Blue and grey are the most usual suit colours, looking smart and flattering skin tone at the same time.

▲ Stronger-coloured and brighter-patterned tweeds are more casual.

great for casual suits or blazers, but avoid them for business wear. In general, the paler and brighter a colour the more casual it is, so if you want to smarten up a linen suit commission, for instance, go for navy rather than royal blue.

Get a paler grey

Most of this applies to greys as well. Too many men wear grey that is very dark, looking more like black with a little texture to it. In fact, there are really two clear categories of grey that can be worn for business: charcoal and mid-grey.

Charcoal is a great shade for business and works particularly well in flannel, but (like navy) it cannot be mistaken for black. Of all the suit colours, however, mid-grey is the kindest on the skin tones of most men – it compliments a good tan, but it doesn't wash out the pasty faced. It is for that reason that I would recommend men creating a business wardrobe (or commissioning their first bespoke suits) to start with in navy, charcoal and mid-grey.

Mid-grey is a touch lighter than the grey suit you would instinctively buy. Don't be afraid – it will look perfectly serious with a blue shirt, dark tie and deep-brown Oxfords. But then it will also work wonderfully in a casual summer setting, with a white shirt, tan shoes and perhaps a white linen handkerchief.

Other colours

A man's next commission should be a blue blazer, and you shouldn't switch to other colours until your wardrobe includes a chalkstripe, a double-breasted, a Prince-of-Wales check and a three-piece.

When you do venture into other colours, the key ones are brown and green. This seems rather daring until you look at tweed, the casual attire of traditional English dress and pretty much always dominant in either green or brown. Both can work in suits or jackets in any material, but remember that lighter colours and stronger colours are more casual. So in a suit, both brown and green should have a touch of the grey about them, and they should be dark enough not to dazzle.

How to pick fabric

There are two common mistakes men make when picking a cloth for their first bespoke suit. The first is the design: it is tempting to choose a fancy pattern and a strong colour, when, as an investment in time and money, it's best to look to something more conservative with your first suit.

Second is the quality of fabric. Most bespoke virgins have been schooled in ready to wear, and make the mistake that the lighter the weight and softer the look the better the quality.

Although a good tailoring house can work with most fabrics, something with a bit of substance and reasonable weight will always tailor and perform best. Do take on board any advice that your tailor gives.

As one's first bespoke suit will be different in fit and cut to what you are used to, keep the design simple. Something plain to establish a cornerstone for your wardrobe, such as a Huddersfield fine worsted in an 11 or 12 ounce weight.

Understanding cloth

When it comes to suit cloths, the material you know is called worsted. That's what 99 per cent of the ready-to-wear suits are made of. It's wool that has been smoothed in the yarn and again after it is woven, to produce a smooth, clean finish. There are many different types of worsted – serge and gabardine are both worsteds yet feel very different – but again, this is a tiny proportion of the cloth on offer.

Within worsted, there are weights to suit every occasion – most of the suits you will be used to from the peg are lightweight, between 9 and 11 ounces. That's a shame, because a man should have variation and even a 14-ounce suit doesn't have to be packed away for the whole of the summer months. There will be chill days when it feels good to slip on a heavier suit, and in a plain grey or navy the trousers may be particularly useful, as trousers are cooler to wear than jackets.

▲ A business man in a suiting advert from 1939 steps out in a traditional heavy worsted.

So try to have a good scattering of weights between 9 and 13 ounces in your wardrobe. If this is your first bespoke suit, you'll probably need something at the heavier end of the spectrum, as the ready-to-wear suits are lighter. That is a blessing, for heavier cloths hang and retain their shape better than lighter ones, so the suit will look even better for it.

Flannel

Flannel is a differently processed and therefore hairier material than worsted. It will feel slightly softer and spongier, but hangs wonderfully and is a great contrast to the shine of a silk tie and polished shoes. (You may also prefer woven ties with worsted suits to continue that contrast.)

Commission a single-breasted grey flannel suit in 12- or 13-ounce cloth and see how it feels to you. Some men prefer it to anything else, as it has such character, and they spend the summer wearing 9-ounce worsted versions that aren't strictly speaking flannel but have that same soft handle.

Others only wear it in autumn and winter and – much like the Italians with suede shoes – feel that there is something about those seasons that suits greater texture. Either way one or two flannel suits are a necessity in any well-dressed man's wardrobe.

Plain tweed

Time was, a man would wear largely tweed or linen at the weekend, as the dignity of business necessitated sleeker cloths during the week. Now in many offices round the world, a man is smart if he wears a jacket of any material. A sharply cut jacket

▼ Flannel is softer than worsted and hangs well. It is also great in contrast to the a silk tie and handkerchief.

in grey Donegal tweed is still a lot smarter than a sweater, so knowing how to wear tweed, linen and all the various incarnations of cotton is important.

Tweed is felted or roughly finished wool that is woven with several differently dyed yarns. It is not just checked wool, as some manufacturers would have you believe. Indeed, the most interesting tweeds are not checked, but distinguished for the number of bright colours combined into a subtle overall tone.

Harris tweeds are woven on the Scottish islands of Lewis and Harris. Tweed of the Harris type generally has one overall colour but many variegated yarns, as described above. Donegal tweed, from that region of Ireland, is distinct in having bigger flecks of a secondary colour, such as yellow in green or white in grey, and is less commonly patterned. Best to start with a classic green Harris tweed for a jacket: single breasted, slanted pockets and probably three buttons. Often the style is of the old hacking jacket used for horse riding, hence it will have a relatively high waist button and a long centre vent.

Do, however, consider a plainer or somewhat more conservative colour for office or general city wear. Grey, pale blue or a very dark green can look just as smart as some worsteds, if cut well and with fewer bright yarns in the mix. Worsted rarely works as an odd jacket, and a cashmere blazer might seem too obvious – in that scenario smart tweed is by far the best choice.

Super numbers

As with bespoke details like working buttonholes, the 'super' number of a suit used to be something that men spent their time boasting about. The higher the number, the more exclusive it was. Super 100s are a measurement of the quality of the wool. It was originally how many centimetres the yarn could be stretched to – so a super-100 wool could be stretched a metre – but has now been codified to refer to the diameter of the wool measured in microns. As a rule of thumb, until your wardrobe is so full that you only wear a suit once every month, stick with super 100s to 130s.

Linen

Linen is the king of summer cloths and for good reason. It is absorbent and dries quickly, taking moisture away from the skin. It is usually in a looser weave than most wools or cottons and therefore allows more air through it. And in heavier weights it doesn't wrinkle and rumple as much as other materials, making it still relatively smart: aim for 13 or 14 ounces.

▲ Most suit fabrics are between super 100 and 130. Higher numbers are finer, but don't wear as well.

Linen is most usually made up for suitings in cream, tan and blue. You may feel that tan is only really appropriate for garden parties or strolling around town on the sunniest of days, in which case go for blue. Navy may look as if you are just wearing a rumpled business suit, so something a little brighter is recommended.

Lapel buttonholes

Traditional bespoke suits should always have two buttonholes in the lapels of a double-breasted suit. They have evolved from military dress jackets, when these would have been working buttonholes and buttoned across the chest in the same way that the other buttons down the forepart do. Indeed for a long time military dress jackets were designed with two foreparts that folded back and buttoned down on themselves – so that if unbuttoned they would have formed a double-breasted with a very large overlap. The lapel, of course, would have been of a slightly different shape, as it would otherwise have been uncomfortable under the chin. The peak that we have today on the lapel is an exaggeration of the shape of old military jackets.

Cashmere

Cashmere is finer than normal wools and so softer, though it is best suited to separate jackets or overcoats – in a full suit cashmere would be heavy and, being soft, not drape as well. Vicuña is from small and rare camel-like creatures. It is even finer, making it very soft but a little sleek as well, and is best kept for luxurious overcoats.

Alternative options

There are some other, minor cloth options you may like to choose from:

MOHAIR is the hair of the angora goat, lightweight but with a slight sheen. This makes it cool but sometimes flashy. Mohair mixes can get the best of both worlds.

HOPSACK is a loose weave of worsted wool that is therefore more textured but also breathable. Particularly good for blazers.

FRESCO is a high-twist, slightly rough cloth that is open and lightweight.

GABARDINE is usually a tight twill in wool or cotton. Good for trousers or a nice alternative to linen in a summer suit.

SEERSUCKER is a ribbed cotton cloth popular in the US. Best to avoid except as a summer jacket.

▲ Cashmere is woven from the wintery down of mountain goats, combed from the animals before it falls off naturally in the spring.

Patterns and surface detail

If you're commissioning your first suit, make it plain. There's enough to worry about with fit, style and colour, don't chuck pattern into the mix as well. But, plain is rarely plain with worsted wools. There are nailhead and pick-and-pick, both of which most men would just describe as plain, and even some herringbone patterns go unnoticed.

In general, a little surface detail is a good thing. Unless the desired look is ultra-smooth and sleek, texture adds to the interest of a suit and contrasts nicely with the shine of a tie, so consider those little patterns to be nothing more than surface texture. Herringbone is often a good option: essentially a broken twill, it adds a touch of interest.

Simple, long stripes

Next are stripes. Most you see these days are pinstripe – a thin line of white or similarly pale colour that contrasts with the background. It's easy to see how to go wrong here – the stripes shouldn't be too strong or too far apart as both appear rakish and that's not a good thing, in business at least. Equally, though, the stripe should not be so dense as to be nothing more than surface detail. It's such a waste. Stripes should always be vertical and should match at the back of the collar and bottom of the pocket flaps. They give an impression of height and therefore flatter short men. Unless you are freakishly tall,

▲ Stripes that are too strong, or too far apart, can be a little flashy, as demonstrated by Frank Sinatra playing Nathan Detroit in *Guys and Dolls* (1955).

Chalkstripe   Prince of Wales

though, they will not look bad on a big man. The
lengthening effect is far greater than the slimming
one – in the end, a fat man in stripes just necessitates
more stripes. It enables the viewer almost to measure
how wide he is.

Another popular stripe is chalk. This is wider but
usually used on flannel, creating a fuzziness to the
line that is both classic and flattering. Try it on a blue
suit and team it with sober accessories. Not rakish,
but certainly full of personality.

Checks

The king of the check is the Glenurquhart plaid,
often reduced to simply glen plaid. This is a check
of several overlapping lines that was made famous
by Edward VII, who created his own version when
he was Prince of Wales. The Duke of Windsor also
popularized it during his travels to the US.
At its faintest, this check is mere surface interest,

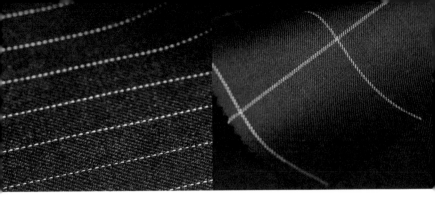

Pinstripe   Windowpane

at its strongest, it is old-fashioned sportswear and unsuitable for business. The difference is really in the tone of the grey (or occasionally blue) that it is set against. Start with a mid-grey and then experiment. The real fun though, is the overchecks. This is a simple, single line that follows the undercheck but outlines it, adding a subtle touch of colour to the pattern. Blue is standard and safe, lime green is surprisingly popular and pink also pops up now and again, but the king is a rusty orange. Try it on your fifth suit.

Lastly, there are windowpane checks. A simple pattern created by single lines, this plaid can again vary enormously in its effect from anonymity to recklessness. A good idea would be to start with a large but faint windowpane on a charcoal ground, perhaps with a peak lapel to echo a little of the rake.

2

Before
Bespoke

Judging the quality of a suit

Price doesn't necessarily reflect the quality of a ready-to-wear suit. It's more indicative of market positioning, branding and a manufacturer's broader costs. But if you're wandering around a shop and want subtly to check the quality of a suit's construction, there are a few easy ways to do so.

Floating canvas

First, and most important, check whether the suit's canvas is floating or fused. Every suit will have a layer of canvas in the chest, to give it substance and structure. This can either be stitched to the inside of the suit, or glued. The latter is cheaper and simpler, but prevents the canvas moulding to the shape of your chest. It can also bubble up under the lapels when wet. To tell whether the canvas is floating or fused, hold the jacket around the waist button, one hand pinching the inside and one the outside. When you pull the two apart, you should be able to feel the canvas in between. If you can't, it has been fused to the front.

Hand-sewn touches

Second, look for handwork under the collar and inside the suit. If you turn up the collar, there is a layer of 'melton' underneath it to give it structure. See if that melton is attached by hand or machine to the body of the suit. (Hand stitches will always be a little bit irregular.)

Then, look inside the jacket. Is the lining of the sleeve attached to the rest of the lining by hand? And is the bottom of the lining attached to the bottom of the jacket by loose, zig-zag stitches (machine, but good), tight regular stitches (machine) or hand stitches?

With all these points, you are looking for elements of handwork on the outside of the suit that suggest more handwork and general care with the inside of the suit. They make some functional difference, but suggest more the attitude to quality taken overall.

Aesthetic buttonholes

Finally, good suits often have their buttonholes sewn by hand. This is largely aesthetic – it makes little practical difference to longevity or ease of use. But it does indicate greater time and effort put into the finishing touches.

▲ A tailor sits on his workbench to baste a new fitting across his knee.

Ready-to-wear sizes

Understanding sizing is key to getting the most out of ready to wear (RTW). The sizes go back more than 100 years. Hart Schaffner & Marx (the company now famous for dressing President Barack Obama) was the first to produce proportioned suits in 1906. It analyzed the male body and broke it down into generic sizes – tall, short, stout and thin.

Standardized sizes

Later, that was refined to categorization by the size of a man's chest. Hence our current system of 38 inches, 40 inches, 42 inches, and so on. The standard had to be about the jacket, as it is so much harder to alter than the trousers, and the chest is the most consistent part of the jacket.

▲ A tailor makes alterations to a RTW suit in 1963.

The waist and length of the trousers, though, were also based on this system. The standard 'drop' today – the difference between a suit's chest measurement and its trouser waist – is 6 inches. So, generally, a 40-inch jacket comes with 34-inch trousers.

If you spend time researching RTW suits, and have two or three points altered, it shouldn't be hard to achieve a good fit. It will never compare to the sculpted look of bespoke, but the suit will fit well – probably better than at least 70 per cent of the male population, which bothers with neither research nor alterations.

Trying on a suit

If a RTW suit is what you want, or is all you can afford, you will need to have parts of it altered. To know what needs to be altered – indeed, to know whether it's worth buying the suit in the first place – you will need to be able to analyze all aspects of fit. So here's a rundown. This will also come in useful later, when we discuss bespoke fittings.

Unfortunately jackets are not simple pieces of tailoring. The way the cloth looks across your back, for example, is affected by everything from the angle of the shoulder seam to the slope of your shoulders, and your natural posture to the height of the waist button. It is not just a question of doing it up and making sure you can breathe.

Start with the waist. This is the fulcrum that the whole jacket has been designed on, anchoring the shoulders and revealing the jacket's structure. Fasten one button and tug it slightly and see how much excess there is. An inch or two is fine. You don't want any stretch lines radiating from the button when it is fastened; but equally it should not be too loose. Unlike a shirt, say, you will undo this button when you sit down (unless the jacket is double-breasted) so the jacket's waist can follow yours quite closely.

Next, look at the length of the jacket. There are many ways to assess whether this is correct, including if it

▲ When trying on a suit, button only the waist button – as above.

The neck should sit flush on your collar. The neck and shoulders are key to the fit of the suit.

The waist button is the fulcrum of the jacket.

The jacket should end halfway down your hands. The length of the jacket should be half the height of the suit.

matches your inside leg. But there are two simpler and more effective ways. Is the length of the jacket (from shoulder to jacket hem) roughly half the height of the whole suit (from shoulder to trouser hem). And does the jacket finish about halfway down your hands, so you can curl your fingers under it?

Of course, many of these points are subject to taste and fashion. Recently the trend has been towards shorter, 'bumfreezer' jackets that recall the 1960 Beatles-era. That's fine if it's what you want, but use these guidelines so you can tell if the jacket is of this style so at least you're making an informed decision. The arms of the jacket should finish around your wrist bone – the point from which your hand flexes. If your shirt finishes at the base of the thumb, this should leave around half an inch of cuff showing (try to wear shirts that fit you well when trying on a suit, if possible).

Most important to the fit of a suit, though, are the neck and shoulders as they are the hardest to get altered. The neck should sit flush on your collar when you are standing naturally (not dead straight as if you are on parade). If it stands away, the collar needs to be tightened; if it is against the neck but there are stretchmarks below the collar, it needs to be loosened. Finally, if the shoulders fit, then the jacket's sleeve should just touch the muscle of your shoulder as it flows down the arm. Your shoulder should not create a bulge in the cloth, but nor should the sleeve hang loose beyond it. It should just touch.

Alterations tailors

Once you've bought the suit, go to the alterations tailor. This isn't a specialist group – for most places in the world today, particularly the US, it is all tailors. (Try to find a good one though.) Alterations tailors regularly shorten the length of trousers and take in the waist. The first doesn't even require the opening of a seam; the second is a simple opening of the waist seam at the back for a few inches, and closing up.

They will also regularly have clients who want the waist taken in on their jacket. Many ready-to-wear suits are made deliberately larger than average in this department. That alteration requires the two side seams on the jacket to be opened – which means unpicking the lining and making sure they get the angle of the alteration even as it narrows towards the scye (armhole) and the hip. But it is a regular procedure and not that technically demanding.

Next on the sliding scale of difficulty is probably shortening the jacket's arms. This can be done one of two ways – either from the cuff or from the shoulder. The latter is far harder as it means detaching the sleeve, shortening it and reattaching, but it is the only option if the jacket has working buttons on the cuff. If the buttons are purely decorative, the sleeve can be shortened from the cuff and the bottom button simply shifted to the top of the row to retain the look. So this is technically more difficult, and should be

Size matters

Many brands and designers subtly tweak the shape they label '40' every season, usually based on fit models hired exclusively for that. Also, given that a 40-inch chest can come in long, regular or short, two or three different styles per line, two or more lines per brand, across many different brands, there are actually hundreds of 40s out there to choose from.

Sizes vary across different continents to account for variations in size among the population. There are also variations within sub-brands. Ralph Lauren's Black Label, for instance, was launched with a seven-inch drop, presuming its prospective clients to be more athletic than Polo or Purple Label. The latter also had a Custom Fit category, which translates as a larger drop.

▶ Altering the neck and shoulders on a jacket, like this tweed one from Neapolitan tailor Elia Caliendo, is a lot harder than altering the waist or sleeve length.

something you think twice about if the jacket is a bespoke or high-grade Italian one. Both are more likely to have a sleevehead that is substantially larger than the armhole it goes into, so the alterations tailor will have to repeat the process of easing in the excess material when he replaces your sleeves. This is not something to be trusted to someone whose prime business is dry cleaning, but while this requires a good amount of skill, it does not require much artistry. The tailor is simply attempting to rewind and then redo an existing process.

Altering the neck and shoulders is different – it's a question of figuration. This is the term for modelling a suit to your physique. Not simply getting the measurements right, but knowing how to pitch the sleeve differently to cope with your posture, or allow more fullness on one side of the back to deal with a prominent shoulder blade.

When a tailor cuts the length of the collar of your suit, so it fits more snugly on your neck, he has the potential to alter all the figuration. Opening the back seam can unbalance one side or the other, pull the front parts of the jacket apart or ruin the pitch of the sleeve so that it hangs forward from your body.

For a good tailor, it is not difficult. But there aren't many of those around. To be safe, as mentioned earlier, always make sure the suit you buy off the rack fits well on the neck and shoulders.

Made to measure

Made to measure will always be a better fit for you than RTW, with many more options to adjust the size to your body. It can drop the shoulders if yours droop; it can narrow the trousers if you prefer a tighter fit; it can even alter the width of the sleeves to cope with particularly bulging biceps.

The fit won't be able to cope with one protruding hip, a slightly prominent shoulder blade or a slight stoop that throws the body forward and ever so slightly to the right. But it will fit very well. It will probably fit you better than 95 per cent of the suits out there fit their owners. It isn't quite bespoke, but it's damn good.

A taste of design

One of the other advantages of MTM over RTW, is that it gives you a little taste of design. Many customers originally seek out bespoke for the superiority of fit, but their interest is maintained by the possibility of design, personal expression and inflicting their personality on the world through the medium of bespoke suiting.

With most MTM orders you will be able to pick the colour and type of the wool, the material of the buttons, the shape of the lapels and the colour of the lining. You will be able to specify the number of pockets, vents and pleats, not to mention cuffs, breasts and buttons. To those with a fascination for men's clothing, this is sorely tempting.

Increasing popularity

MTM has become increasingly popular in recent years, with many high-street brands that you wouldn't otherwise associate with tailoring introducing the service. This is essentially an easy way for them to jump on the bandwagon of a tailoring revival. As men become interested again in how their jackets fit, they want more than a standard block. MTM enables the brands to offer a little more – using the same fabrics, the same trimmings and perhaps even the same factory that produces their normal suits. The additional manpower is minimal, it just needs a certain number with enough expertise to get the measuring right (too many brands fall down on this point – if you've ever tried out a mail-order suit service where you or a friend has to take your measurements, you'll know how hard it can be).

Staying with a brand

Returning to the point about design, the advantage of this growth in high-street MTM is that customers can still get the style and cut they like from the brand they like. New companies or tailors are at risk; men like to stick with what they know.

The loose style of Fred Astaire

Fred Astaire was known for the relaxed, easy-going feel of his clothes. He ensured that the armholes on his jackets were always cut high and tight, to give his arms greater freedom to move without dragging the rest of the jacket with him. He famously jumped around the fitting room at his tailor Anderson & Sheppard, stopping suddenly to glance in the mirror and check his collar was still tight to the back of his neck.

Astaire's clothes were not cut loose to help him dance. Rather, he wore larger clothes because he wished to hide his slim physique. Whenever one sees images of him, it is notable that his neck, wrists or ankles are always very thin compared to the volume of his clothes. It is a credit to Astaire's tailors that this never looked out of place or attracted attention.

Recommended retailers

There are some wonderful ready-to-wear suit makers out there. Their value is largely in design and cloth, aspects of the suit on which bespoke tailors will always struggle to compete with the top designers. But having recommended 'designers' quite broadly, I would advise you always to avoid the catwalk type unless aesthetics are your only consideration. Construction-wise, they will nearly always be the worst value for money.

Among the better RTW suit makers are Kiton, Brioni and Tom Ford. All very expensive but of good quality.

These few brands may seem like a small number. But if you remove all the high fashion (some well made but never worth the money on quality alone) and the high street brands, there are a few good ones left.

Brioni

FLAGSHIP STORE: 38–40 VIA DEL BABUINO, ROME

WWW.BRIONI.COM

Also has branches in London, Tokyo, New York and a handful of other places outside Italy. Brioni is not for the faint-hearted. Its prices for suits regularly top those of the most expensive bespoke tailoring establishments. The quality of the workmanship is extremely high, with many aspects like buttonholes being sewn by hand, as well as the collars and sleeves being attached by hand. But the amount of handwork is never going to be as high as the bespoke tailors.

▼ Actor Jon Hamm sports a silk houndstooth tuxedo from the Brioni Spring collection at an Oscar's afterparty in 2016.

Tom Ford

FLAGSHIP STORE: 845 MADISON AVENUE, NEW YORK

WWW.TOMFORD.COM

The biggest arrival in luxury menswear for 20 years. Once Tom Ford launched his eponymous label on leaving Gucci, he quickly became famous in the

industry for researching the very highest possible qualities of cloths and manufacturing possible, from one-piece leather jackets to hand-cut suits. The price tags are big and aspirational and the cuts aren't for everyone – they are masculine, big-shouldered and big-lapelled. The patterns, too, are strong and hard to pull off. But the quality and mastery of colour and tone is superb, and this would be the place to go for a tuxedo. Dozens of stores worldwide, sprung up in double-quick time.

Kiton

FLAGSHIP AND SHOWROOM: 11 VIA GESU, MILAN
WWW.KITON.IT

Although lesser known outside Italy than Brioni, Kiton is just as luxurious and no less expensive. Specializing particularly in ultra-lightweight worsted cloths and fine cashmeres, its style is typically Neapolitan: soft jackets with a lot of drape, with little structure or canvas; shoulders are natural and often have the sleeve sewn underneath the shoulder, like a shirt. This contrasts with the more classic shape of Brioni. Kiton is also well known for its bright colours in summer and experiments in cloth and tone. Stores in 11 countries.

Loro Piana

FLAGSHIP STORE: 27C VIA MONTENAPOLEONE, MILAN
WWW.LOROPIANA.COM

Luxurious casualwear for the off-duty Italian. Loro Piana is famed for its cashmere, becoming the first house in the world to offer baby cashmere – combed from the young goats in their first spring, it produces a tiny amount of wool that is two microns finer than normal cashmere. Like Zegna, Loro Piana has also done much to protect the vicuña camelids in South America. The company produces knitwear and blazers, as well as all manner of other clothing items and accessories (and its own cloths for tailors, at least as fine as Zegna). Watch out for the Storm System label in some items – this is a wind- and rain-proofing fabric patented by Loro Piana and often used by other brands. A few dozen stores worldwide.

Ermenegildo Zegna

FLAGSHIP STORE: 27E VIA MONTENAPOLEONE, MILAN
WWW.ZEGNA.COM

As a cloth manufacturer, the house of Zegna is virtually unsurpassed in all the world. It still makes most of its money out of supplying cloths to other tailors, or making suits with those cloths for brands like Tom Ford. Its retail offering is very mixed. At the bottom end it competes with the likes of Canali and Corneliani. At the top end it makes pieces that compare with the big Italian luxury names for handwork. Make sure you know which you're getting. There are hundreds of stores worldwide, in every major city, and in 27 of the 50 US states.

Rubinacci

FLAGSHIP STORE: 149E VIA CHIAIA, NAPLES
WWW.MARIANORUBINACCI.NET

A Neapolitan tailoring house that has become famous for its use of colour – particularly as worn by the third generation of the family, Luca Rubinacci. Rubinacci offers bespoke tailoring around the world (as do Brioni and Kiton) but is increasingly well known outside Italy for its accessories and ready to wear. Luca launched a successful range of ready to wear and accessories for the first time in Autumn/Winter 2010.

Ralph Lauren

FLAGSHIP STORE: RHINELANDER MANSION, 867 MADISON AVENUE, NEW YORK

WWW.RALPHLAUREN.COM

Simply the most consistent purveyor of the classic American style there has ever been. And by classic American, we mean everything English with American inspiration thrown in. Polo, but with Long Island arrogance. Ralph Lauren's quality, too, is often very high – even Polo suits usually feature loose sewing of the linings, something few other mid-range suits bother with. As with Zegna, there is a lot of variation in retail though. Hundreds of stores around the world.

▲ Ermenegildo Zegna's flagship store, Milan.

3

The Bespoke Process

Getting measured

Having clothes made by a tailor can be a frustrating business. Truth is, few of us are any good at designing clothes. That's what makes the retail experience satisfying: browsing designs and being inspired by something that we love but would never have imagined. Other people design for us. However, once you know all the elements of fabric, style and pattern you're in a much better position than most. You know how many buttons you want on your jacket and why, which type of wool and in which weight. All that's left is to master the fitting process itself. Get it right and you'll bespeak something as good as retail. And after two or three attempts, you'll create something better.

Usually, a tailor will discuss cloth with you first, before getting out the measuring tape. Little details like pockets and buttons may come later, but he'll want to get a sense of the weight and style of suit first. A Norfolk jacket fits differently to a sharp, navy worsted for example. Then it's on with the measuring. Once the tailor gets going, the number of measurements may seem bewildering.

On the trousers, for example, he'll need the inside and outside leg; the waist, hips and seat; and then the thigh, knee and cuff. And the jacket is much more complicated. Just stand still and let him do his job – but bear a few of the following things in mind.

First, stand naturally. One of the greatest arts of tailoring is arranging the back parts so they fit smoothly all the way up your back, resting evenly across your shoulders and fitting snugly against the back of your neck. No off-the-peg suit will do this. It will always be a little too tight or loose at the neck and rest unevenly on one shoulder. This is because off-the-peg suits are made for an average stance, with no lean forward or back and neither to one side or the other.

And no one is average. Everyone stoops a little bit; everyone has one shoulder that drops slightly more than the other. So don't try to hide this from the tailor, stand as naturally as you can, and try to relax. Shake your arms out; roll your neck; take a breath, and let go. Then try to stay in that frame of mind for the next 15 minutes or so.

Secondly, anticipate the aspects of fit that the tailor will not know from looking at you. How long do you like your sleeves? It helps if you wear a shirt that you like the fit of – then he can refer to the amount of exposed cuff rather than to your wrist bone. How long do you like your trousers? Again, wear something you are already quite satisfied with. The beauty of bespoke is that there will be at least three more occasions after this for you to express your feelings on tightness and looseness. And it's much easier to give your opinion on an actual jacket than in the abstract. So just give some rough indicators to the tailor. Grunt approval, shrug or wrinkle your nose. He should get the message.

The basted fitting

The next stage is the basted fitting. This may be anywhere from three weeks to two months after the initial appointment. Between first and second fittings, the cutter that measured you up will have cut a series of paper patterns approximating the pattern of your suit – front and back panels, sleeves, collar and trousers. He will then either have cut out the wool himself – by laying a pattern onto two layers of the cloth – or given it to a 'striker' (undercutter) to do so. A basting tailor will then roughly sew all the pieces together. The lines are not rough, but the stitches are long and loose, so that after your basted fitting they can be ripped out and the cloth re-cut.

Putting on a basted jacket is a slightly odd feeling. It doesn't look like the suit you envisaged. It has no structure, has white stitches all over it and may only have one arm. Do not panic. The basted fitting is all about fit, not style. If your tailor is any good, he will spend most of his time looking and marking, rather than asking questions. He's analyzing how the cloth falls across your back, deciding that one or other shoulder has to be a little lower, that there is too much drape under the arm or that the collar has to be higher. Alterations will be chalked on, for the guidance of his shears later on.

▶ A basted fitting for a bespoke suede jacket. A baste will often not have the sleeves attached, or they will be removed during the fitting.

From your point of view, consider the elements of fit you can see. Is the sleeve you do have too long or

too short? The tailor will have pinned the front of the jacket closed at the waist – does this feel too tight or too loose? Remember to move a little (when he is not about to pin or chalk you). A jacket should be comfortable when you are walking and stretching, not just standing still.

It's easiest to tell how a suit is put together when you see it at the basted stage. That first fitting shows the various parts of the jacket – two back parts, two foreparts, collar and the front and back of sleeves – sewn loosely together so the tailor can get an idea of the fit and then easily take it apart again to be re-cut. Those are the outer parts. Then you have the lining to the body and the sleeves. It is usually made today of Bemberg (rayon) or Emerzine (viscose); these allow the wearer to slip the jacket on and off easily. Other than perhaps some slight insulation and structure, that is their sole purpose. The sleeve lining will usually be white with alternating coloured lines, no matter what the lining of the body. Some tailors have house patterns for the sleeve that they always use and can identify their work.

Canvassing

Within the chest there will be one, two or three layers of felt, wool, cotton or horsehair in some combination. A standard English suit will have a layer of horsehair running all the way behind the forepart of the suit, with a layer of felt and canvas in the upper half. Those are sewn loosely together with basting stitches and then attached, again loosely – though securely – all the way around the edge. The

horsehair is very flexible, stretches and moulds easily. So it will shape to the contours of your chest after a few wears, creating a three-dimensional shape that fits you in a way the tailor cannot build for. This 3D shape is one of the reasons it is important to hang, press and pack your jacket carefully.

▲ Unfinished suits revealing padding and interior structure at Brioni in Pescara, Italy.

Because the felt and horsehair is only tacked at the edges, it can move or 'float' within the suit. This is the floating canvas that is referred to as the hallmark of a good suit. Poorer products will glue (fuse) the canvas to the forepart, reducing its ability to move and mould.

Variations on structure

More layers and different materials can be used to create greater shape to the jacket. In the opposite direction, it can be cut down in size or removed altogether to reduce structure. The unlined suits discussed above obviously do not contain any canvas. Half-lined suits usually do, but even fully lined suits can just have canvas down to the waist, in order to reduce weight and make the jacket more breathable. Coats equally – it is rare to find coats today that are fully lined, right down to the hem. It is one reason that vintage coats tend to be so much heavier. It makes them much more wind-resistant though.

Other structural elements

Other structural aspects of the suit include the collar and shoulders. The collar is pretty similar to the chest – a layer of canvas and one of melton, sewn loosely together and then attached to the back of the neck. There is more variation in the shoulders, though they will tend to follow the same philosophy as the chest. So an Anderson & Sheppard style suit will have less shoulder padding or, at the least, it will be of a softer, spongier material.

The wadding at the top of the sleevehead (the shoulder of the suit beyond the seam that attaches it to the sleeve) can also vary. More wadding creates a 'roped' shoulder that stands higher – giving the impression that there is a strip of rope running around the shoulder. Extreme versions and padding can lead to a 'pagoda' shoulder that actually curve up, leaving the line of the wearer's shoulder entirely.

De-structured suit

When Giorgio Armani famously de-structured the suit in the early eighties, he both reduced the weight of the canvas and cut it down in size (as well as making the whole suit baggier).

Italian tailors had been doing it for years, driven by the need to cope with higher temperatures than those in England.

Most Italian suits today will tend to have less structuring. It's easy to tell how much canvas there is and how far it stretches – just pinch the forepart on front and back and feel the layer in between.

Richard Gere's clothing in *American Gigolo* (1980) really put Giorgio Armani on the map.

The forward fitting

At the next fitting, often called the forward, the most obvious things that will be missing are the buttons and buttonholes. This is because any alterations that have to be made at this stage are much easier if buttonholes have not already been cut. If one sleeve has to be shortened, for example, it can be done by taking cloth off the end; if the buttonholes were already sewn, the sleeve would have to be detached from the shoulder and shortened at that end. The forward fitting is the first time you will see your suit in something approaching a finished form. You will be able to see how the design is going to work, how much space will be left for the tie and where the gorge (the seam between the collar and lapel) will sit.

Look the suit up and down and consider every aspect. Are you happy with the jacket length? Are the pockets the right height and straight/slant? Is the waist tight enough, does it flare too much into the skirt? The forward fitting is meant to avoid any alterations on the finished suit, so your tailor should be happy you're spotting so many things at this stage. Of course, far more important is that the tailor pick up any last points of fit, such as the balance across the shoulders and line through the waist. Changes should be minimal and final. Your pattern will be altered to incorporate these, so that in the long term a suit is nearly perfect as soon as it is cut and you can skip at least one of these fittings.

Final alterations

A few weeks later, you should have the finished suit. Still think of this as a fitting, though, especially if it is your first from this tailor. Don't go to the appointment expecting to walk away with your suit. Chances are there will be something small you don't like, and much better to pipe up now then come back with the suit in a week or so.

Common things that often need changing at this stage are the length of sleeves and trousers. The other alterations made after the forward fitting always seems to tweak one or both of those. And both lengths are crucial to a well-fitting suit.

The finished suit

So after another week or two, you should have your finished suit. But again, don't think about this as the end of the process. As you wear the jacket it will mould to your chest and fidget until it sits naturally on your neck.

Go back, get any little things seen to somewhere down the line. And bear them in mind for the next suit. It may take a long time to get to perfection, but the steps get smaller and smaller.

Soft versus structured

Tailors like Anderson & Sheppard in London use two layers of lighter weight wool or cotton, to soften their suits. Equally prestigious Huntsman on Savile Row is famous for a more 'structured' look and uses a thicker canvas.

Proponents of the soft approach (including Steven Hitchcock, son of Anderson & Sheppard's head cutter John Hitchcock, and ex-A&S cutter Thomas Mahon) would say their suits are more comfortable. Proponents of the latter (including ex-Huntsman head cutters Richard Anderson and Terry Haste) would say theirs flatter the customer more.

Each is merely a question of taste. If you want a comparison, all are usually open to going into the shop to try on or at least see standard garments. (Indeed Huntsman also offers ready to wear, so there is a ready selection of models to try.)

Subsequent suit commissions

Once you have commissioned a few suits similar in style from one particular tailor, you have a choice to skip either the basted or forward fitting. This is not to cut corners; rather it is the next step in bespoke, once you are happy with the shape you have achieved with one particular tailor. At this stage his pattern for, say, a single-breasted jacket on you should be pretty much cemented. The balance should work well, the sleeves will have been adjusted to just the right length and small issues like the height of the waist button have been ironed out. So it makes sense to speed the process up. Effectively you would normally have three fittings: basted, forward and final.

Fit or design

Really though, the choice comes down to whether you are more confident in the fit of the jackets or in their design. The basted fitting is mostly about balance – it is the tailor's opportunity to get the figuration right and re-cut the cloth if anything is wrong. The forward fitting helps too, but it is mostly about you seeing the design in its near-finished form. It is not too late to alter the button positions or the roll of the lapel, or to spot any mistakes. You may not be bad at designing suits, but take it as a given that your tailor is a lot better at fitting them. You may have designed perhaps a dozen or so; he's cut hundreds. So if you plan to skip one, make it the basted fitting.

The fit of bespoke trousers

At some point during your first session with a tailor, he will ask you what length you like your trousers to be. While there are guidelines for this, it is also a question of taste. Give your opinion on the length, then try sitting down. Again, it is important that they are comfortable when you are moving, not just standing still. Cloth can be taut but should not constrain.

The traditional length is such that the trousers fall on your shoes with no break in the crease at the back – it is a straight, uninterrupted line from hip to heel – and in the front there is a single break (fold). This is roughly the same length as the trousers would be if you stand in your socks and the back crease just touches the floor. This standard length will make your legs appear long and sleek, with no interruption in that elegant line at the rear. Others are also unlikely to see much of your socks as you walk along.

However, the trend in recent years has been for shorter trousers. While designers like Thom Browne have taken it to extreme lengths, many brands and tailors have tended towards the short. But short trousers are not a recent phenomenon. A particular strain of southern European men, particularly in Milan, have always worn their suit trousers short. Usually they will wear their trousers so they just touch the top of their shoes – no break in the front as well as the back.

If you want to echo this tradition of shorter trousers, I recommend going for turn-ups (cuffs). It helps that they, too, are more fashionable than they used to be. And of course it is easy to reverse that decision later. However, if you want something more conservative and less likely to be noticed, go for a single break in the front. Perhaps a shallow break, just to give your shoes a little breathing room.

The lap seam

Lap seams are an anachronism that still have a few followers in bespoke circles. They were originally used to add greater strength to a join, and they are more substantial. But today they are used for style, to subtly highlight the line of the leg. They are generally used on the side seams of trousers and involve leaving a little flap of cloth, lying flat and facing backwards, down the seam. In a way they are an exaggerated version of a raised seam, where both pieces of cloth simply overlap and are sewn together (what you get down the inside of a pair of jeans). With a lap seam, both pieces are sewn together, folded over and then sewn down, leaving a little excess cloth, or 'lap'.

▲ Standard length trousers with a single break.

Where should trousers sit?

In my opinion, there are really only two options on the waist of your trousers – either it sits above your hipbone or in its hollow. The first will probably require braces. This is the traditional height – it will be around the same place as your waist button on the jacket and is better with pleats (to flow out and over those hipbones). As it will be on the middle of your stomach, it is also more comfortable with braces – braces allow the waist to be a good inch wider than normal, as tension is not required to keep them up.

The second position is what 99 per cent of young men wear today. Not slack, not drooping halfway down the bottom, but sitting across the hips and definitely below the stomach. The most important thing is that the position feels natural to you and does not alter as you move around the fitting room. If it does change, the length will be ruined – and that is the part of a pair of trousers most constantly on display.

Sew superior

The best bespoke suit will be made by hand, allowing flexibility and attention to detail in key areas of the suit.

Attaching the lining to the inside of the suit by hand, for instance, allows it to move when you do, without disturbing the cloth outside so that your silhouette remains smooth and sharp.

You can tell if the lining has been done by hand by looking at the point at which it joins the bottom of the back part. Machine stitches are tight, small and very regular. Hand stitches may still be quite regular, but there will be tiny variations and bigger gaps. The shoulder seam also benefits from handwork, allowing it to stretch slightly as you move and reach.

Hand sewing also means the tailor can use silk thread where needed, which is stronger than the normal cotton used by sewing machines.

Finally, with hand sewing, a large sleevehead can be fitted into a small armhole, which allows a man to move his arms freely without disturbing the fit of the rest of the suit.

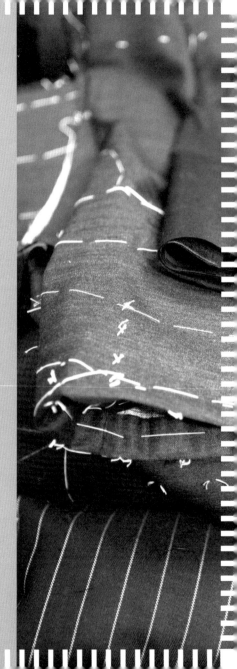

Recommended bespoke tailors

No one has tried every tailor on Savile Row. Most that can afford that level of bespoke stick with just one, and only move if their cutter leaves or retires. Some continue to patronize more than one, but they are the minority. Their experience is very limited among the 20 or so bespoke tailors on and around the Row. Once you go off Savile Row, the number doubles or triples – even more once you venture into the City. This is, of course, not counting visiting tailors that have their suits made elsewhere.

All this is a roundabout way of saying that the following list is necessarily subjective. It is built on personal experience, reputation and the many recommendations of peers. Consider this a cumulative recommendation, but no guarantee. Unfortunately for one's bank balance, the only way to truly find a tailor you love is by trial and error.

United Kingdom

Anderson & Sheppard
32 OLD BURLINGTON STREET, LONDON
WWW.ANDERSON-SHEPPARD.CO.UK

Known for its soft structure, Anderson & Sheppard is one of the best-known names on the Row. Its distinctive shape is inherited from Frederick Scholte, the revolutionary tailor who pioneered soft tailoring through a more natural shoulder and lighter chest padding, cut on the bias for greater movement. The relatively new premises on Old Burlington Street are also among the best of any Row tailor, exuding both tradition and modern elegance.

Steven Hitchcock
11 ST GEORGE STREET, LONDON
WWW.THESAVILEROWTAILOR.CO.UK

Steven Hitchcock is the son of Mr John Hitchcock, ex-head cutter at Anderson & Sheppard, and the man who has cut several superb suits for me. His son's reputation is very strong, and many visit him for a slightly different (and slightly cheaper) take on the Anderson & Sheppard look.

Thomas Mahon
14–16 MARKET PLACE, BRAMPTON, CUMBRIA
WWW.ENGLISHCUT.COM

Another ex-Anderson cutter, Thomas Mahon's cut is soft and comes highly recommended. Being based in the north of England, Thomas is cheaper than anyone on the Row, although he still does most of his fitting and client appointments there.

H. Huntsman & Sons

11 SAVILE ROW, LONDON

WWW.HUNTSMANSAVILEROW.COM

Huntsman has reigned supreme at the heart of
Savile Row for 160 years, in its own words. Whether
it has reigned exactly is rather subjective, but it is
certainly among the top few houses for tradition
and reputation. The classic Huntsman shape is
rather different to Anderson & Sheppard – a strong
shoulder, greater padding in the chest and a nipped
waist. Single-breasted jackets usually feature a single
button. It is more upright, military and to that extent,
flattering than soft tailoring. Although if you prefer
a softer structure to a suit, the tight little stitches
of Huntsman can seem a little constricting. Unlike
Anderson & Sheppard, Huntsman offers both ready
to wear and made to measure, so you can wander
into the shop and try on a suit to get an idea of the fit.

▲ Tailors hard
at work in the
basements
beneath
Huntsman's
showrooms.

Richard Anderson

13 SAVILE ROW, LONDON

WWW.RICHARDANDERSONLTD.COM

Richard Anderson was briefly the head cutter of
Huntsman, and the youngest man to hold the
position, before he left to start up his own shop down
the road. The house cut is consequently similar to
Huntsman, though Richard has a reputation for more
adventurous styles and a glamorous clientele. Expect
an openness to innovation and suggestion.

Henry Poole

15 SAVILE ROW, LONDON, WWW.HENRYPOOLE.COM

Henry Poole, while not the first tailor on the Row,
certainly founded the reputation that it has to this
day, and for that reason is old-school royalty amongst
the tailoring fraternity. It is the only firm still to be
family owned and family run, with the line passing
from Henry Poole to his cousin, Samuel Cundey, at
the end of the nineteenth century and Angus Cundey
still among the directors today. While Huntsman
always had a reputation for being the most expensive
shop on the Row (now no longer true), Henry Poole
has always been quite modestly priced compared to
its neighbours and yet loses nothing to reputation for
tailoring excellence.

Norton & Sons

16 SAVILE ROW, LONDON, WWW.NORTONANDSONS.CO.UK

Norton & Sons was revived a few years back by one
Patrick Grant, a dashing business graduate who has
succeeded in that short time in not only putting life
back into a great tailoring name but also launching a

ready-to-wear fashion line that now has its own store in London (E. Tautz). Nortons & Sons was always most famous as a tailor of hunters and adventurers, and at one time created several new ways of keeping a British explorer dry, warm and elegant at the same time. Today the suits are of a structured shape with a firm shoulder; unique Scottish tweed is also a particular strength.

Jonathan Quearney

7 WINDMILL STREET, LONDON
WWW.JONATHANQUEARNEY.COM

Jonathan is another example of a soft-tailoring advocate, but tucked away from the rest up on Windmill Street. He was trained by Thomas Mahon but has developed his own unique, contemporary shape and style. He is fascinated by craft but also has a peculiar gift for colour, always emphasizing how customers have to be shown the coloured weaves in even the most basic-looking grey or blue suits. Having set up his own shop, he has proved successful at communicating that soft approach to a new generation of bespoke customers. Recommended for those looking for a younger take on a classic cut.

Graham Browne

12 WELL COURT, LONDON, WWW.GRAHAMBROWNE.CO.UK

The only City tailor listed here (located in the business district of London), Graham Browne is a well-kept secret that I stumbled upon a few years ago. Recently rekindled by head cutter Russell Howarth, previously at military tailor Kashkets, this shop just off Bow Lane near to Bank station is possibly the best-value bespoke to be found anywhere in London. And unlike many tailors, Russell is always open to suggestion and experimentation – as evidenced by my odd requests and his work with Guy Hills of Dashing Tweeds.

North America

Leonard Logsdail

9 EAST 53RD STREET, 4TH FLOOR, NEW YORK
WWW.LEONARDLOGSDAIL.COM

Leonard Logsdail is an Englishman in New York. He originally trained on Savile Row, under Bernard Wetherill amongst others. (Wetherill was relaunched by Kilgour in 2010, as a separate bespoke house with a slightly different, hunting take on tailoring from the clean, modern aesthetics of Kilgour next door.) Today Len is based in midtown Manhattan, and has a charming little establishment shared with tailor and RTW-purveyor Stephen Kempton.

Paul Stuart Custom

MADISON AVENUE AT 45TH STREET NEW YORK, NY 10017
WWW.PAULSTUART.COM

The wonderful Paul Stuart store on Madison Avenue has been offering its version of custom tailoring (as the Americans call bespoke) for several years now. The process is exactly the same as bespoke, but pre-made chest pieces are used (padded by machine instead of by hand). The results, with a rather draped style, are very elegant.

Francesco Pecoraro, LeatherFoot

82 AVENUE ROAD (YORKVILLE), TORONTO,

ONTARIO, CANADA M5R 2H2

WWW.LEATHERFOOT.COM

Italian tailor Pecoraro has been in Toronto, Canada for decades, catering to a small local clientele. It was only in April 2016, however, that he came to wider prominence when he moved his workshop into the newly expanded LeatherFoot store. His soft, southern Italian style is complemented by a roped-shoulder option that offers a stronger silhouette.

France

Camps de Luca

16 RUE DE LA PAIX, PARIS, WWW.CAMPSDELUCA.COM

One of Paris's two great tailoring establishments. After forging a reputation in Milan, Mario de Luca teamed up with Joseph Camps, who was revered across Paris for his originality and invention. He was the showman to Mario's diligent, management character. Today the shop is run by Mario's son and grandson, Marc and Charles de Luca. The house has a reputation for a sharp silhouette and little innovations like a tear-shaped inside pocket.

Cifonelli

33 RUE MARBEUF, PARIS, WWW.CIFONELLI.COM

Cousins Massimo and Lorenzo Cifonelli now run this establishment, having started in the workshop in 1993 and taken over in 2003. They say the house style combines the best of English, French and Italian tailoring: flair, strong structure and precise detailing. Cifonelli now also offers MTM and RTW. The jackets all feature the typical strong and forward shoulder, as well as some great details like exterior pockets on the sleeve and curved patch pockets.

Italy

A Caraceni

VIA FATEBENEFRATELLI, 16, MILANO MI, ITALY

WWW.A-CARACENI.COM

A Caraceni in Milan is probably the best known of the bespoke houses that came out of the Caraceni family. With a spotless reputation, Caraceni is still considered one of the best of all Italian tailors. It is currently run by Carlo and Massimiliano Andreacchio, and their softly made but square-shouldered style is popular among businessmen looking for something that looks formal but feels weightless on the body.

Ferdinando Caraceni

VIA S. MARCO, 22, MILANO MI, ITALY

WWW.ARACENISARTORIA.COM

Bizarrely enough, Ferdinando Caraceni was no relation to the rest of the Caraceni dynasty that has influenced tailoring across Italy. But he was the cutter at Domenico Caraceni and then Augusto Caraceni for 29 years. Today the shop is run by Ferdinando's daughter Nicoletta, who keeps her father's traditions alive with a small team.

Liverano & Liverano
VIA DEI FOSSI, 43, 50123 FIRENZE
WWW. LIVERANO.COM

The biggest and best-known tailor in Florence,
Liverano cuts quite a distinctive style: slightly shorter
jacket, cutaway fronts and a broader lapel. They
have become popular in recent years off the back of
The Armoury. Visit their stores in Hong Kong and
New York.

Rubinacci
(FOR DETAILS SEE PAGE 66)

Mariano and Luca Rubinacci run a large and
impressive tailoring house in Naples – and between
them have brought bespoke tailoring to a new
audience around the world. Luca in particular, with

his idiosyncratic style and fondness for bright colour, has become an online celebrity in recent years. More conservative dressers look to the subtler but no less powerful style of Luca's father Mariano.

Panico

VIA CARDUCCI, 29,80121, NAPLES

WWW.SARTORIAPANICO.IT

Like many tailors, Antonio Panico is getting on in years, and may not be around much longer to cut his beautiful, distinctive double-breasted jackets. But for the moment, he has one of the best reputations in Naples and is always worth a visit.

Caliendo

VIA S.MARIA DI CAPPELLA VECCHIA , NAPLES

WWW.SARTORIACALIENDO.COM

Although not as well known as the likes of Panico and Rubinacci, Sartoria Caliendo is a very strong tailoring outfit with a large customer base in London. Founded by Biaggi and now run by his son Elia, the house is particularly strong on quality finishing – something not all Neapolitans prioritize.

Hong Kong

A-Man Hing Cheong

5 CONNAUGHT RD, MANDARIN ORIENTAL HOTEL, HONG KONG

The atmosphere at A-Man is friendly, clubby and collegiate. The dark wood interior puts customers at their ease and regular clients frequently pop by to run through fittings or flick through cloth books. Most Hong Kong tailors don't have much of a house style, but you could certainly make an argument that A-Man does – a fairly classic English shape, with some structure to the chest and shoulders. It also tends to favour English cloths. Compared to its close cousins below, A-Man also tends to use fewer details like horn buttons.

W.W. Chan

UNIT B, 81F, ENTERTAINMENT BUILDING, 30 QUEENS ROAD
CENTRAL, HONG KONG, WWW.WWCHAN.COM

Both W.W. Chan and H. Baroman are old Shanghai tailors, established in that city early in the twentieth century and only relatively recently having arrived in Hong Kong. Known back then as the red gang, these tailors set up an apprentice scheme that trained many of today's master tailors. Along with A-Man Hing Cheong, these two in particular have become firm favourites with visiting sartorialists from the US and UK. Not cheap by any means, but approaching Savile Row standards for a considerable discount.

N

**SANDOWN
SABLE**

58 59

**SANDOWN
SABLE**

60 61 62

57

**SIC
MA**

**CLASSIC
PANAMA**

58

**CLASSIC
PANAMA**

60

**ASSIC
NAMA**

**CLASSIC
PANAMA**

59

**CLASSIC
PANAMA**

61 62

5 56

CHESTER
GREY

NAMIBIA

N

57 58 59
60 61 62

56 57

4

Finishing
Touches

MIAMI
SAN

RIV
PA

L
H
S.J
H

S M L XL

56 57

S M

MIAMI
BLACK

SAVANNAH

SA

S M L XL

58 59

60

Suit linings

▲ Italian sports jackets, such as this from Stile Latino in Naples, often have brighter or patterned linings.

Most suits will be fully lined, but they can be half lined (also known as 'buggy lining'), quarter lined or even unlined. Mostly this is done to save weight and increase breathability in summer suits. A half lining stops at the side seams, leaving the back exposed save for one or two sections across the neck to make it sit cleanly. A quarter lining stops halfway to the side seam. Although jackets with less than full lining require less material, they usually take longer to construct and so can be more expensive. Within the cloak of a lining a tailor can get away with a multitude of sins with his seams and loose threads.

As your lining is made of the same material as your tie (well, a similar one, silk is rarely used today as it doesn't breathe well and manmade fibres last better) and contrasts with the suit cloth in the same way, the process of colour selection should be the same. Except that you can't change your lining. So think about it like this – if you could only ever wear one tie with that suit, what colour would it be?

Don't be afraid to get a bright lining if you are not driven by a transitory trend. Bright red has long been a classic accompaniment to navy, for example, from socks to scarves. So a red lining in a navy suit is not necessarily trendy. However, if you want colour, it's generally better to stick to dark but unusual tones – rich, deep shades of purple, green, blue and burnt orange. Think of the choice in the same way you think about your tie. The tie colours that really draw admiration are not flashy yellows but purple with navy, orange with brown, a green with mid-grey flannel. Other colour combinations I recommend are gold or copper with grey, bottle green with blue and purple with charcoal. With tweeds, bright colours often work very well, probably because most will have some bright colours woven in there, in however small a quantity.

If you want to be safe, though, go with a lining that is similar to the suit. Like your socks rather than your tie – same colour, perhaps a touch darker. This is the lining that no one will notice, and is definitely recommended if your suit is otherwise quite striking. A bold check, for instance, or contrast buttons. It's all a question of balance.

Follow a similar philosophy for lining patterns: only be as bold as the suit will allow. Beware, though – if anything a bold pattern can appear cheaper than a bold colour. Avoid polka dots and paisley designs, unless very subtle.

▲ A lining similar to your suit material, even if brighter, is usually a safe option.

Other lining options include football strips – famously incorporated into suit jackets by some tailors. Or indeed shirtings – although not as slippery as silk-like materials, they work well enough in a half-lined jacket or just to tape the seams of unlined jackets. The thin strip used as tape means a bold pattern can become a subtle suggestion.

Selecting your buttons

There's plenty to consider when it comes to buttons: number, material, colour. Buttons can be fun to shop for and there are some great online sources. Few, however, will stock matching sets in the sizes required for the front and cuffs. Make sure they do before you buy. Buttons should always match. The buttons of most good suits are made of horn from animals such as cows, deer or buffalo. They're tougher and tend to have richer colour tones than plastic or corozo. Having said that, they make little overall difference to a suit and if there were one thing you could sacrifice in a jacket it would probably be horn. (Followed by handmade shoulder pads and some hand sewing. At the other end of the scale would be bespoke fittings – never give them up.)

Blazer buttons can be experimented with and gilt versions are the most classic. Avoid a crest unless it is yours or your club's, school's or college's. Personally I dislike the associations with gilt-buttoned blazers and prefer alternative high-contrast colours such as white, cream or silver. Covered buttons, where the cloth of the jacket or lapels covers the button entirely, are most common on dinner jackets. Other natural materials to shop for are shell and wood. Mother-of-pearl buttons are standard on good shirts, but they can also look good on pale jackets, and black versions equally on high-shine materials such as mohair or silk. Wooden buttons give heft and texture (rather

like leather, another option when braided for odd
jackets). In general if opting for unusual materials, it
is advisable to go for a slightly darker tone than you
would otherwise.

▲ Button storage
at G.D. Golding
tailors, St
Albans, UK.

On Savile Row, tailors will often match buttons to the
cloth they go with. So a navy suit will have dark-blue
buttons, a grey suit dark-grey ones. Like a matching
suit lining, they tend to be similar but ever so slightly
darker. Paler buttons can't help but look cheap.
However, there isn't that much variety to be had
with grey or blue. By far the nicest horn buttons are
in brown. From darkest chocolate to palest chestnut,
brown horn buttons will contain more variations
in tone and swirls of pattern. And if you usually wear
brown shoes with your suits rather than black,
I highly recommend brown buttons.

Buttonholes

The best bespoke suit will be entirely made by hand, and that should also include the buttonholes. You will be able to tell the difference as the stitching will be visibly rougher on the inside.

Cuffs can have one, two, three, four or five buttons – even none if that's the look desired. Four is standard, and I would avoid three. Five is for when extra decoration is desired, while two is old-fashioned and one fashion-forward. Turn-back cuffs will generally have two buttons or none at all.

▶ Most suit jackets will have four cuff buttons, while sports jackets often have three.

Working buttonholes used to be a sign of bespoke clothing. The buttons on your cuffs would actually undo all the way up, allowing you to wash your hands without getting the cuff wet. Ready-to-wear jackets hadn't done it for years, so those that did had to be bespoke. Men would undo the first of these buttons as a subtle indication of bespoke. Then about 10 years ago, ready to wear started including working buttonholes alongside other design details such as coloured stitching and hand-stitched lapels. Suddenly these things weren't a sign of bespoke, quite the opposite. Interestingly, Anderson & Sheppard traditionally made its suits without working cuffs. So to them it was never a sign of bespoke.

The standard pockets

Pockets – so easy to appear so dull. Not many options, you'd think. But a suit can come alive with the pockets.

If you want a standard suit, and the tailor asks you what pockets you require, tell him: two outer hip pockets, straight and flapped; one plain outer breast pocket; two inner breast pockets; and probably one internal ticket pocket. This last is the small pocket on the inside left of the jacket that was probably used originally for tickets; today it is sometimes used for change but, most often, contains business cards. Such are the evolving needs of society.

Normal hip pockets are bags sewn into the inside of a jacket. If you have an unlined jacket you can see them hanging there, often tacked to the inside so they don't snag. The outer opening, a slit, is covered by a flap. This is largely to make its appearance cleaner, as otherwise the slit can sag and look unattractive.

▲ A normal hip pocket is covered by a flap to make its appearance cleaner and neater.

Welt pockets

However, a pocket without a flap (called a besom or welt pocket) is common on dressier outfits such as a dinner jacket. It used to be common on normal suits in the twenties and thirties as well, but then suits were made of such thick stuff that a flap added greater proportionate bulk.

Today welt pockets can remain as clean, crisp slits if they are rarely used to contain anything. Some tailors would recommend keeping them basted up to make sure they never sag. Indeed, some men do this with all their pockets, flapped or welt. It dissuades them from ever putting anything in there. A good alternative is to have smaller sections sewn into the inside of the hip pocket, perhaps split into two across the pocket's width.

The outer breast pocket is not flapped, but has an extra strip of cloth sewn across its front instead. This is the pocket your handkerchief should go in – arranged in a casual, degagé air; in fact just stuff it in there. Some patch pockets have a similar design, with a strip across the top to give them bulk.

Patch pockets

Patch pockets are a simpler design, created by sewing a patch of material onto the outside of the jacket rather than a bag onto the inside. If welts are more dressy, patches are more casual. They are most often found on the more casual type of jacket – summer, tweed and hacking, for example.

▲ The outer breast pocket can be a welt or patch – as above. It is perfect for your pocket handkerchief.

On a suit jacket they are an easy way to make it appear more casual and, perhaps, make it suitable for wearing separately. The cloth must be casual (thick or rough). Another thing that helps that impression is the addition of an external ticket pocket. This is most usually positioned above the right hip pocket (presuming the wearer to be right handed) and is narrow but deep, in order to suit a vertically slotted

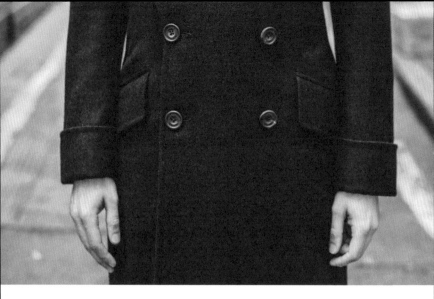

▲ Slanted pockets are set on an angle. They originally designed to be easier to use while on horseback.

ticket. Appropriate on any style of suit really, but definitely a casual design element.

Experiment with shape

All our pockets so far have been straight. They can also be slanted or even curved. Slanted pockets were originally conceived to make access easy on horseback. As a result they are common on hacking jackets today. On suits, however, they are seen as dressier than straight pockets, as the diagonals create a sharper look. Curved pockets are a lovely eccentricity, but should be reserved for tweeds and gun club jackets.

Additions to the suit

While this book is definitively about suits and not the things that are worn with them, it is worth saying a few words on the various connections.

Shirts

As with black tie, the style and formality of a shirt is worth considering in relation to the suit it is being worn with. It looks rather odd to sport a corduroy suit with a white, spread collar and double-cuffed shirt. Go for a tattersall or an Oxford cloth instead, and single cuffs.

The fit of a shirt should also parallel that of the suit in a few ways. There's little point having a trim jacket if the shirt underneath billows at the waist – the effect is rather undermined when you take the jacket off. And a jacket with a high armhole should be worn with a similarly tight-holed shirt to take full advantage of the extra movement this design allows.

Handkerchiefs

My favourite accessory. The outer breast pocket always looks rather naked – or pointless – without something in it so I recommend at least a white linen square. Silks are for wearing with rougher cloths or when one is not sporting a tie. Too much silk otherwise. The only element of wearing a handkerchief that is relevant to a suit is that a lower buttoning position on the jacket will mean its lapel overlaps the pocket slightly. I like this – the handkerchief should peep. If the buttoning is higher,

the pocket and thus its handkerchief can be rather isolated. If you decide you like that effect, it is worth bearing in mind when you design your first bespoke suit.

Ties

Ties are really a question of style rather than fit. From printed foulards through various wovens into square-ended knitted ties, there is a formality scale that should be mimicked in the suit. But one thing that is worth bearing in mind with the 'fit' of a tie is that the front blade should finish on the waistband of the trousers; the rear blade should be the same length or, if that's impossible, a little longer. Some very sartorial gentlemen even tuck that rear blade into their trousers. Whatever your height or personal style, the length of your tie is obviously related to where you wear your trousers and is therefore worth considering in bespoke.

Seven-fold ties

Different ways of counting folds have become confused, and today any multi-fold tie (more than three folds) is often called a seven-fold tie.

Most normal ties have three obvious folds. If you look at the back of the front blade, the silk has been folded in on itself on either side, and one of those flaps has just been tucked under creating a small, third fold. While retaining the same width of those two sides, the silk can be folded in on itself almost as many times as you like. You just have to start with more silk, and the tie becomes thicker. The folds go right through the tie (or do on a good one) and can be seen on the back blade, though this might be hard to see as the first folds will be quite high up inside.

You can spot a real seven-fold because for a tie to have an uneven number it must either have a little lip like the three-folds or the folds must overlap and concertina into each other.

Accessory retailers

Albert Thurston

WWW.ALBERTTHURSTON.COM

The best maker of braces, or suspenders, anywhere in the world. Not many men today wear braces, but for those who do I can't recommend anywhere more highly than Albert Thurston. Stored by tailors everywhere, but also available on the company's website. Worth trying on first, however, to make sure you get the right length. The most popular style involves the excess hanging down in front of the waistband, and you don't want that too long.

Charvet

28 PLACE VENDOME, PARIS

As a silk trader and former visiting shirtmaker, Charvet knows its cloths and manufacturing details. The headquarters in Paris is a must-visit and, as well as the shirts, I highly recommend their ties, which knot especially well despite their standard construction. Also carried in many department stores, such as Bergdorf Goodman and Selfridges.

Drake's

3 HABERDASHER STREET, LONDON, 3 CLIFFORD STREET, LONDON, WWW.DRAKES.COM

A relative newcomer to the world of retail, Drake's has for a few years been making ties for the biggest names around the world – all by hand, all at the company's workshop in London. Since launching itself online,

both ties and scarves (the company's starting point) have been very popular. Key to the success has been the colour sense of director Michael Hill.

▲ Turnbull & Asser, gentleman's outfitters, St James's, London.

Dunhill

BOURDON HOUSE, 2 DAVIES STREET, LONDON, WWW.DUNHILL.COM

Although the leather luggagemaker has become somewhat more over the years, with its own series of 'houses' now around the world, I particularly recommend Dunhill for its accessories. Silk handkerchiefs are tasteful and well made, silver cufflinks are a standby and the leather goods are worthy of any man's investment. Look out for the

Alfred Dunhill collection, made by hand at a factory in north London – where the company's famous pipes are also handwrought. Other branches in almost 50 other countries worldwide.

Kiton

(FOR DETAILS SEE PAGE 65)

Always worth visiting for shirts and accessories. The shirts, you will notice, are hemmed by hand, creating a seam along the bottom that most resembles a well-rolled handkerchief. Also known for little innovations such as ties made out of a single piece of exclusive worsted suit cloth.

Lock & Co

6 ST JAMES'S STREET, LONDON,
WWW.LOCKHATTERS.CO.UK

Founded in 1676 to serve the court of Charles II down the road at St James's, Lock & Co is a British institution. The distinctive white hatboxes are still stacked around the walls, the staff as polite and deferential as ever and the quality of the headgear is still the finest you will find. I recommend the travelling fedora, complete with a tube version of the hatbox to roll it up in.

Rubinacci

(FOR DETAILS SEE PAGE 66)

Accessories aplenty here in surprising colours and combinations. Silk scarves and handkerchiefs featuring scenes of Naples; scarves flamboyant in Aztec-like designs; umbrellas made by Brigg but personalized for Rubinacci with bright colours and polished knobs of wood. Seven-fold ties with the lightest of linings too, as well as knitted ties in unusual colours as popularized by the son of the current owner, Luca Rubinacci.

Tom Ford

(FOR DETAILS SEE PAGE 64)

As with suits, shirts and much else, the quality of Tom Ford's merchandise is impressive and I would recommend the accessories as highly as the ready to wear. As you would probably expect, the patterns are often bold but the colour schemes subtle enough to push the accessory into the background. For those that like a thick blade and a long knot, the ties will be the best you can find.

Turnbull & Asser

71 & 72 JERMYN STREET, LONDON,
WWW.TURNBULLANDASSER.CO.UK

T&A is now one of the very last vestiges of great shirtmaking on Jermyn Street. With its own factory in Gloucester, and its own exclusive cloths, this is shirtmaking as it used to be. The reputation is for relatively stiff shirts with floating collars but reinforced points and plackets. And the reputation for rather adventurous colour is also well deserved, although T&A can still make you a wonderfully soft Oxford button-down in plain unadventurous blue. T&A is also a general purveyor of everything from suits to sweaters, in the Jermyn Street mould; but I'd prioritize the shirts above all else. T&A also have branches in New York and Beverly Hills.

5

Occasionwear

Rules for black tie

A man's dress used to be driven by social propriety – what his peers considered to be fit and proper. Most of the rules for dress that we have inherited were formalized by social norms. Style icons were made when those that could broke with convention and wore new combinations, such as Edward VIII wearing suede shoes and double-breasted jackets. He made that acceptable – but he was not necessarily the first to do so, just the first to sufficiently encourage others to follow his lead.

Today, there is little of this social propriety left. Men in some offices know they have to wear a suit and smart shoes. Some social fixtures, such as race meetings, have dress codes. But that's about it. Today the only area where men know their dress is prescribed is when wearing a dinner jacket, or black tie.

However, common mistakes are still made with black tie. The biggest is that a man's waist is often not covered. With black tie you have three options: waistcoat, cummerbund or double-breasted jacket. All cover the waist and conceal that part of the shirt. They are listed in declining order of formality (unlike most other areas of dress, double-breasted is considered less formal than single). This choice then goes some way to determining the shirt a man wears. Most evening shirts have stiff or starched fronts in some shape. A small or oval front is designed to sit

under a waistcoat, so only that part of the shirt is exposed when one's jacket is open. A cummerbund leaves more of the shirt exposed and must therefore be worn with a wider stiff front in a rectangular shape. Being less formal, it may also be worn with a pleated front and turned-down collar. Stiff-fronted shirts most often have a wing collar, though this is not universal.

The second mistake men make is to mismatch the formality of waist covering, shirt front and collar. Each is on a sliding scale and must not be too far apart from the others.

The third biggest mistake men make is wearing black tie during the day, something the Americans are particularly guilty of. Black tie is evening wear. The jacket should have a peaked collar, rather than a notch or step. This reflects the outfit's antecedents in the morning and frock coats. A shawl collar is acceptable but is more casual. It is often found on double-breasted or smoking jackets – or indeed more casual dinner jackets like a tropical-weight ecru, famously worn by Humphrey Bogart in *Casablanca*.

While black tie is generally black, it can in fact be midnight blue, brown or any other dark colour. Noel Coward had a brown outfit, complete with matching tie and pumps, made for him by Douglas Howard. Some rakes of the past have worn dinner jackets in all the colours you commonly see smoking jackets in today. However, generally only the first of these alternatives – midnight blue – is recommended.

A touch of individuality

There are areas of the black tie ensemble where you can add a touch of your own individuality – know the rules, then twist them: that's the motto here.

Shoes

Shoes for black tie should be, at the least, highly polished black Oxfords. The Oxford is cleaner than the Derby, and so more formal. Brogueing is also informal, so shouldn't be worn with black tie. While black Oxfords are fine, patent is better for being that bit shinier. The whole of the black tie ensemble is about contrasting textures – wool of suit with silk of lapels, seam on trousers or shine of bow tie. Patent enhances that contrast. And although many men don't like the artificial finish, a delicate patent shoe with a thin, cemented sole is really much smarter.

Formal white

Counterintuitive though it may be, there is nothing wrong with wearing a white bow tie with black tie. The adjective does not refer to the colour of the bow tie but to the overall dominant colour of the outfit. However, a man today is likely to be castigated by the ignorant for wearing a white bow tie. So instead, try wearing a white waistcoat in the same stiff Marcella material as your dress shirt, instead of a black one that would echo the jacket. Again, a white waistcoat is not wrong, merely more formal. And a white

waistcoat will ultimately stand out far less than a
white bow tie.

Most white waistcoats will be backless, with merely
a collar and elastic at the waist. Both white and black
can be made as such, and it is far more comfortable;
the device was probably invented originally by
shirtmakers Hawes & Curtis.

Keep the jacket on

Of course, it goes without saying that you would
never take your dinner jacket off, so the back of the
shirt would never be revealed under the waistcoat.
Indeed, black tie is the outfit that demonstrates
this maxim of menswear better than any other.
Every item, from the waistcoat to the shirt to the
cummerbund, would lose its elegance if the jacket
were removed.

There used to be a tradition of patterning the
non-display parts of one's shirt with humorous
motifs, like animals or cartoon characters, merely
to demonstrate this point. But that goes down as
needlessly loud and garish personality, hidden or not
– why would a man ever want his black tie attire to
be humorous?

The little extras

Black tie is so simple, the little extras can be important for the outfit.

Handkerchiefs

For evening, it is natural for the handkerchief to reflect the lustre of the bow tie, lapels and trouser seams, rather than contrast with them, so choose silk, worn in a puff. The easiest way to achieve this is to take one corner of the handkerchief and stuff it into your pocket until it reaches the bottom. Then take the opposite corner and stuff it behind the first one, carrying on stuffing the body in until only a couple of inches of puff are on display. The fact that one corner is touching the bottom will prevent the handkerchief slipping down.

As for linen, there is certainly licence here to be more decorative than during the day so fold it into a three or four-point arrangement: fold each corner up until it is beside the top one, clustering the four together. Then fold in the sides and stuff it.

You could have a little colour here. Certainly have it in the handkerchief rather than the bow tie or cummerbund. Good colours for a silk pocket handkerchief could be scarlet, purple or gold. Anything that looks rich and luxurious, preferably with some delicate pattern.

Boutonniere

The other option is to have colour only in your boutonniere. The flowers, often carnations, lilies or roses, should be neat and secured with a loop of thread behind the lapel. Red is best, but also yellow or white. Perhaps a deep-red clove carnation or a hybrid tea rose in white.

Bow ties

A bow tie should be one that you tie yourself. If you wear a wing collar, it should also be sized to your neck so that no join is visible at the back. Get a size bigger than the shirt you would normally wear, as it can always be made smaller by tying a little more loosely. Generally though, the aim is to tie the bow tie securely but not too neatly. It should be obvious that it is not pre-tied – not because you want to show off, but because a little *sprezzatura* is always more elegant.

There are other finishing touches you can apply to black tie, but they should always be of secondary importance. Pocket watches in the waistcoat are nice, though nicest with a fob in the middle. A smart topcoat in black – perhaps with a velvet collar or at least peak lapels – is also a pleasant addition. A silk scarf or cane seems rather excessive. The last three are harder to justify given that no one at the event will see you wearing them.

Occasionwear suppliers

Favourbrook

MENSWEAR: 55 JERMYN STREET, LONDON ACCESSORIES:
19–21 PICCADILLY ARCADE, WWW.FAVOURBROOK.COM

Favourbrook is the only establishment in London where one can find excellently tailored occasionwear from the classic to the frankly frivolous. From fancy waistcoats to made-to-measure morning suits, Favourbrook is a great resource for inspiration – I recommend a quick trip for ideas in the run-up to any big event. For greater discretion, experiment with pale colours and subtle detailing, such as a sugary pink waistcoat with lace embroidery.

Brioni

(FOR DETAILS SEE PAGE 64)

Brioni had long dressed James Bond as played by various actors, until Tom Ford took on that responsibility for Daniel Craig. That is just one of the reasons that men associate Brioni with great evening wear, the others being its reputation for incredibly elegant yet lightweight suits.

Budd

1–3 PICCADILLY ARCADE, LONDON
WWW.BUDDSHIRTS.CO.UK

A mere matter of metres away from Favourbrook's waistcoat selection is Budd – a traditional shirtmaker through and through. It doesn't do email; it doesn't do slim cuts. But it makes some of the best bespoke dress shirts to be found anywhere in the world. Classic stiff, detachable, wing collars are not easy to find today: so many are poor, short, flimsy imitations. Budd will have the right thing, together with some great accessories. Ask to see the bespoke shirtmaking upstairs if you get a chance.

Charvet
(FOR DETAILS SEE PAGE 112)

As listed elsewhere, an excellent source of all shirting and accessories, for occasion as much as business wear. Dress shirts, bow ties, silk scarves: I recommend describing your desires to the sales staff and letting them guide you. Worth the trip to Paris on its own. From London, anyway.

Tom Ford
(FOR DETAILS SEE PAGE 64)

Tom Ford has sold his brand on sex appeal and it is therefore no surprise that the dinner jacket, with its suggestion of meetings in the night, cuts a special dash when styled by Mr Ford. Expect sweeping lapels, a nipped waist and the closest thing you will get to an Atlas silhouette. Cloths, too, are a source of brash experimentation for those who want it. There are bow ties (large), cummerbunds and velvet slippers (high-heeled, high-waisted) to match.

Peckham Rye
11 NEWBURGH STREET, LONDON, WWW.PECKHAMRYE.COM

It's an old rhyming slang phrase for 'tie'. And it's a small and relatively modern-looking establishment best known in the UK for its skinny neck ties. But for occasionwear look past the ties towards the silk scarves, which are amongst the very few in the UK still to be made – most importantly, fringed – by hand. For the evening they have white silk ties, both plain and spun to feel like cashmere. I particularly like those faced with both types of silk, one on each side, to hang casually around the neck on the way to an event.

Henry Poole

15 SAVILE ROW, LONDON, W1S 3PJ

WWW.HENRYPOOLE.COM

Anyone on or around Savile Row will cut you an excellent black or white tie. I would simply recommend that you go to whoever you have the greatest experience with and faith in. The only reason I pick out Henry Poole here is that I have personal experience of their velvet jackets. But fit and therefore the expertise of your own tailor is paramount.

James Smith & Sons

53 NEW OXFORD STREET, LONDON

WWW.JAMES-SMITH.CO.UK

Many storied establishments will sell you a great walking stick to accompany white tie. Swaine Adeney & Brigg would be another recommendation. But little compares to the experience of going into James Smith & Sons, that slightly ragged, rather dusty establishment at the end of the Tottenham Court Road. Lack of frills means value for money. And with a little pressing, great service to make sure your exacting needs are met. I highly recommend them for umbrellas.

Pumps and slippers

The ultimate footwear for black tie is black pumps with a silk bow. These look like open-topped shoes, a little like ballet pumps. But they have a bow across the top that, like one's bow tie, should match the lapels of the jacket (usually grosgrain silk, rather than satin). Unsurprisingly, many men don't like pumps. But with the most formal versions of black tie, they are correct.

Velvet slippers, at first glance, may appear to be similar. But they're actually at the other end of the formality scale. Created to be worn around the home, they are casual and best paired with informal black tie such as a velvet smoking jacket, which again was often worn for entertaining at home (once general formality had slid to the point that a dinner jacket was standard outside the home). Velvet is a soft, homey material – wear the slippers and the jacket together.

6

Possess

Suit maintenance

The most important things for suit maintenance are nothing to do with cleaning or pressing, but what you do with the suit when you take it off. Whether cleaning or storing a suit, or just hanging it up in your wardrobe, you need to take care to retain the shape and avoid damaging the fabric.

A bespoke suit has a very specific three-dimensional shape that has been designed to fit your body. When it is not hanging on that body, and moulding its chest to yours, it needs to be draped around something that is similar in shape. This is most important for the shoulders, because their dominant line is horizontal while the rest of the suit is vertical. They suffer the most when a suit is just dropped on the floor.

Hanging up a suit

So the first thing you need is a hanger with decent shoulders to it. This means that the two ends of the hanger must be as wide as possible. It is good if the breadth of the hanger from end to end is similar to your own; never use a woman's hanger for a man's jacket or vice versa. Equally, it is nice if the hanger can be in a natural wood, so it absorbs and deodorizes any moisture accumulated during wear. However, neither of these things are as important as just hanging up your suit every day. Get home, take off your jacket; lay it on the bed, fold the trousers and hang them carefully; then repeat with the jacket.

Make sure that the suit has a little breathing room in the wardrobe, to avoid creating new creases. Don't hang it on the back of a chair, whatever shape. That is most likely to distort. If you don't have a hanger, fold the jacket carefully in half and lay over the bed or chair.

If hung well, trousers should retain their crease for quite a while. When it needs firming up, either use a trouser press or an iron – just make sure to set the latter on a low heat and put a tea towel on top of the cloth. Direct heat will create a shininess in the wool.

Packing a suit for travel

When you're travelling with a suit, it helps if you have a suitcase that is as long as your jacket. To pack, turn the jacket inside-out, making sure to pull through the shoulders. Fold the collar up and, holding the jacket by the reversed shoulders, fold it in half. Lay it in the suitcase and make sure it is packed securely all around. Because the inside of the jacket is facing outwards, there is less risk of nicking or otherwise damaging the wool.

If you don't have a suitcase that large, fold the jacket again lengthways, at a point just below the waist button. This should mean you are not folding the external pockets, which are hard to fold neatly. Trousers are simple to fold, though again it helps a lot if you have a suitcase that is as wide as half the trousers' waist. If you don't, fold the trousers into thirds and place in the centre of the case.

Cleaning and care

As with shoes, it helps the long-term upkeep of your suit immensely if you brush it down at the end of every day. A soft clothes brush, briefly passed over the jacket and trousers, will remove surface dirt and dust that is all around us during the day and gets into the fibres, wearing them down.

It's good to do this every day, but not essential. You might not always be bothered to do so, after a night out, for example, though that's still no excuse to leave the jacket on the floor either. Just try and brush as much as you can – far better to do it irregularly than not at all.

Dry cleaning

Everyone dry cleans their suits too often. If you could see how dry cleaning is done, you would avoid it like the plague. The suit is spun around in a vast drum, mixing with chemicals, and then pressed in an equally large machine that squashes the whole thing flat. Not good for the three-dimensional chest or shoulders, as mentioned previously. In fact, it can ruin the good work your tailor has done to make the jacket fit. What's more, the chemicals don't so much get rid of the dirt as dilute it and spread it around. When you do get the suit dry cleaned, use a professional. Who counts as a professional? Well, I would say someone that also steams and presses a suit – which is what you should be doing in between dry cleaning.

How much to dry clean?

There is some disagreement about how often you should dry clean a suit. Everything from once a month to absolutely never. Despite being aware of the dangers of dry cleaning, some men declare it necessary because men are just messy, particularly in the bathroom. An occasional sprinkle is inevitable. Others retain never dry cleaning as a point of absolute principle. Those men tend to be older and, in my experience, are unlikely to sponge and press their suits much either.

Realistically, it depends on how you wear the suit and how often. The range should be between every six months and every five years, depending on those factors. If you wear the suit once a week to work, perhaps keep the trousers on when you get home, and never go out clubbing in it, then being dry cleaned once a year should be fine.

Seasonal clean

Many men have everything dry cleaned before they put it away for the season – packing away their summer linen and getting out the winter flannel. That's certainly the right way round to do it: never pack things away dirty.

Steam and press

A steam and press involves a gentleman (historically, one's valet) pushing steam through the cloth in much the same way that an iron does, though not as fierce or as close, and then using an iron to smooth the cloth back to perfection. He will use various curved blocks to do this on, so that the chest, shoulders and sleeves retain their impeccable three-dimensional shape.

If you dry clean your suits once a year, have them steamed and pressed once every three months (assuming the kind of wear described on page 135). It is particularly nice to do this when you return from travelling, as all packing will create some creases. Most good hotels will also provide this service for you when you arrive at your destination.

Recommendations

One good tip I was given for finding a steam-and-press man was to find the Four Seasons hotel in a particular city and ask them where they send their dry cleaning. I've tried this twice in large cities, and it has worked. Always best to have a personal recommendation.

Seasonal storage

When one gets to the luxurious stage of having too many suits to hang comfortably in a wardrobe, it's worth thinking about ways to store them effectively over the spring/summer season, and then over autumn/winter. This doesn't necessarily mean having two exact sets of clothes – there can be overlaps, most suits are at least two-season. But it makes sense to put away overcoats, gloves and heavy sweaters during the summer, as well as the heavier tweed and flannel suits. Equally, summer cloths like linen and cotton could effectively be put away for the winter.

Store all items clean, so any dirt is not worked into the cloth and doesn't attract mould or infestation. Fold carefully and separate with tissue paper if you have any. I tend to store in my suitcases, but if you can do so in another environment that is clean and dry that is preferable (and easier). Then have everything pressed by a professional when it comes out. And if you get to the stage of storing shoes as well as clothes, you've really made it.

Share and discover

As with so many of the world's niche obsessions today, there are several style forums and blogs where you can find out more than you ever wanted to know about bespoke tailoring. There are personal experiences, geeky arguments and pages and pages of 'shoe porn' – where fans post pictures of their favourite shoes, from revealing angles.

As a reference tool, they are invaluable. If you need first-hand reports on tailors or brands, just type it into the search function and you'll find a myriad of ratings and rantings. Equally valuable is information on little known styles, tailoring quirks or points of historical interest.

Among the Internet resources, there are three major forums: 'Style Forum', 'Ask Andy About Clothes' and the 'London Lounge'. Although the first two are theoretically American and the third European, in practice contributors come from all over the world and are often participants in more than one. AAAC was founded by Andy Gilchrist, who offers his own guide to clothes and the 'London Lounge' by Michael Alden.

There are many more blogs in the US than in the UK or Europe, many of them obsessed with preppy style. Among the best are 'Ivy League Style' and 'The Trad'. In the UK, the biggest is 'Permanent Style'. But I will pass no comment on its worth, as it is my own.

Although not really a blog and not dedicated to classic style, Scott Schumann's 'The Sartorialist' is a constant inspiration. Nowhere will you find better pictures of Italian classicism and Swedish eccentricity. Books are much simpler. There aren't many great ones out there, but by far and away the best of dressing well is *Dressing the Man*, by Alan Flusser. And for a history of the suit, with cracking illustrations, go find *Sharp Suits* by Eric Musgrave.

www.styleforum.net
www.askandyaboutclothes.com
www.thelondonlounge.net
www.ivy-style.com
www.parisiangentleman.co.uk
www.permanentstyle.co.uk
www.thesartorialist.com

Glossary

6x4 An arrangement of buttons on a double-breasted jacket where, of six buttons on the jacket, only four ever appear to be fastened. The remaining two are show buttons. So 4x4 has four, of which all four appear to fasten, etc.

Basting Sewing with loose, long stitches. Usually used to make parts of a jacket easy to disassemble. Hence a basted fitting.

Bird's eye A pattern of small regular circles.

Buggy lining A half lining to a jacket, with nothing on the back of the jacket save one or two sections across the shoulders.

Canvas The inner construction of a suit's chest, usually consisting of a layer of felt and a layer of woven horsehair or wool.

Cashmere The long, fine hair that hircus goats grow through the winter. Combed off by herders in the spring before it falls off naturally. Very soft and most often used for overcoats and odd jackets.

Chalkstripe A wide stripe on cloth with a little nap, creating a blurred effect. Pinstripe is thinner and sharper; bead stripe is made up of small dots.

Coat Traditionally, what we now call a jacket: the upper half of a suit. Still called that name by Savile Row tailors. Hence an overcoat goes over the coat. Today, an abbreviation of overcoat.

Collar Section of the jacket directly above the lapel. Different to the lapel in that it is attached separately. The join of the two creates a notch, peak or fish-mouth lapel.

Corduroy Ribbed cotton, originally used as a substitute for velvet. Now used for casual trousers, occasionally odd jackets.

Cuffs Also known as turn-ups, the turned up strip of cloth at the end of a pair of trousers or jacket sleeve.

Flannel Wool without the treatment of worsted, fuzzier with a greater nap.

Flat front Trousers without pleats.

Forepart One half of the front of a jacket, from buttons to side seam. The corresponding part of the back is the backpart.

Fork The area where trousers' inside seams meet.

Forward fitting Usually the second fitting for a suit, where all parts are connected but await finishing touches. Easier to change aspects of fit than with a finished suit.

Glenurquhart plaid A check, often referred to as glen plaid, of several closely packed lines. Often with an overcheck.

Gorge The point at which the lapel and collar meet.

Herringbone Essentially a broken twill, creating a zig-zag pattern.

Hopsack A loose weave of worsted wool that is therefore more textured but also breathable.

Horn The traditional material for suit buttons. Made from the horns of animals like cow, deer or buffalo.

Houndstooth Also known as dogtooth, an exploded (enlarged) weave of contrasting colours that creates a jagged pattern.

Midnight blue A very dark blue.

Mohair Goat hair often used for suitings to be lighter and breathable. Has a slight sheen and therefore sometimes used for evening wear as well.

Nailhead A pattern on cloth of small, regular dots, similar to the tops of nails.

Odd jacket A jacket not worn with matching trousers. Also known as a sports jacket or sports coat.

Pagoda shoulder One where the shoulder line curves slightly upwards.

Paper pattern The plan of a suit that a tailor creates from his measurements. Transferred onto cloth with each new suit, and altered over time as the customer changes.

Pick and pick A weave to cloth that reveals more of the interwoven colours, such as black and white in a grey.

Rise The distance from the fork of a pair of trousers to the waistband.

Roped shoulder One with a raised top to the sleeve.

Scye The armhole of a jacket that the sleeve attaches to.

Seersucker A ribbed cotton cloth popular only in the US.

Skirt The bottom half of a jacket, below the waist.

Strap and buckle Also known as side straps or side tabs, buckles on either side of the trousers' waistband that tighten them.

Suitings, coatings, shirtings Cloth used to make each of those items of clothing.

Super 100s A measurement of the fineness of worsted wool. Originally a measure of how many centimetres the yarn could be stretched to, now codified by the diameter measured in microns.

Tan A pale, caramel-type colour.

Tape A thin strip of material used to close seams when the lack of lining means they are exposed.

Trews Trousers made of one piece of cloth per leg, so neither has a side seam. Often used with checks so they don't have to be matched up at the side.

Tweed Felted or roughly finished wool that is woven with several differently dyed yarns. Not just checked cloth.

Twill A cloth woven into fine cords, usually running diagonally across the cloth.

Waist The slimmest part of your body, between your lungs and hipbones. Around or just above your belly button. As a result, the slimmest point of a jacket and where the waist button is usually positioned. Also often used to refer to the top of trousers, even if worn on the hips.

Windowpane A large check of single lines at least two or three inches apart. When the horizontal and vertical lines are different, a Tattersall check (usually on shirts). Over another check, an overcheck.

Worsted A treated and finely woven wool, what the vast majority of modern suits are made out of.

Index

This edition published by
Hardie Grant Books in 2016

Hardie Grant Books (UK)
52–54 Southwark Street
London SE1 1UN
hardiegrant.co.uk

Hardie Grant Books (Australia)
Ground Floor, Building 1
658 Church Street
Melbourne, VIC 3121
hardiegrant.com.au

Copyright © Elwin Street Productions Ltd
2016

Conceived and produced by
Elwin Street Productions Limited
14 Clerkenwell Green, London, EC1R 0DP
www.elwinstreet.com

British Library Cataloguing-in-Publication
Data. A catalogue record for this book is
available from the British Library.

Cover illustration: Clare Turner
Interior design: Fogdog.co.uk

ISBN: 978-1-78488-097-2

Printed in Malaysia

10 9 8 7 6 5 4 3 2 1

MIX
Paper from
responsible sources
FSC® C012700
www.fsc.org

FSC is a non-profit international organisation
established to promote the responsible
management of the world's forests. Products
carrying the FSC label are independently
certified to assure consumers that they come
from forests that are managed to meet the
social, economic and ecological needs of
present and future generations, and other
controlled sources.

PICTURES: Alamy Stock Photo:
© AF archive, 77; © Andrew Cowie, 90;
© Brian Harris, 89; © Chloe Johnson, 70;
© Christopher McGowan, 42; © Chronicle,
36; © EDB Image Archive, 106; © Interfoto,
61; © Jeff Gilbert, 99; © Jorge Royan, 128;
© Julia Hiebaum, 115; © Keystone Pictures
USA, 119; © Mark O'Flaherty, 63; © Peter
Horree, 114, 126; © Peter Scholey, 113;
© REDA &CO srl, 67; © Tony French, 46, 85;
© WENN Ltd, 65. Luke Carby: 20, 95, 105,
116, 120, 125. Crollalanza/Rex/Shutterstock:
15. Jamie Ferguson: 7, 9, 10, 12, 18–19, 21, 22,
25, 29, 30, 31, 32, 35, 37, 38, 41, 44–5, 49, 51,
52, 57, 68, 73, 83, 87, 100, 101, 107, 108, 110,
111, 129, 139. Horst Friedrichs: 27. Getty
Images: Archive Photos, 43; Bruno Vincent,
13; Charley Gallay, 64; Jill Ferry Photography,
130; Lambert, 50; Oli Scarff / Staff, 103;
Michael Ochs Archives, 17; Philip Lee Harvey,
55; Vincenzo Pinto, 75. Jack McDonald: 71,
80. LeonardoModa.com: 40. Paul Stuart
Custom: 92. Shutterstock: Dinga, 137.